RED PANDA ACTIVITY

Can't think what to do?

1000 SUPER FUN ACTIVITIES

Fill in the missing numbers on the balloons. Hint: Multiples of 5.

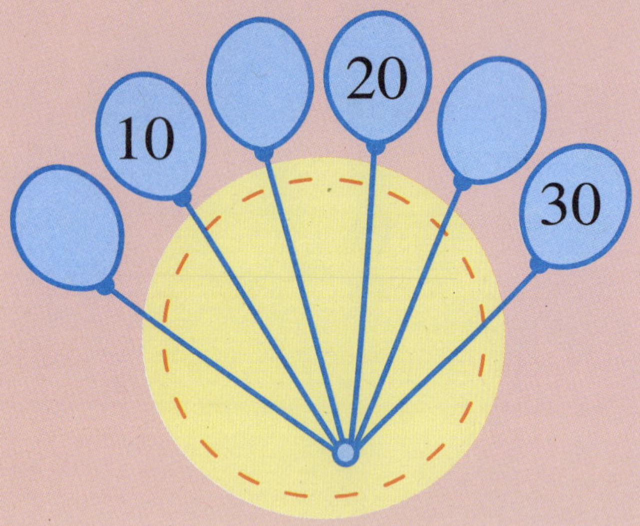

Connect the dots and colour the picture.

Fill in the missing letters to complete the names of the toys.

T_u_k

T__dy

Number the images in the correct sequence.

Find the bigger one in each pair and colour it the same as the smaller one.

Match the objects that go together.

Find and circle two identical images in each row.

Help the little bird find the way to her eggs.

Complete the drawing and color it.

Colour 2 strawberries from each row, so that their numbers add up to the number on the leaf.

Colour to reveal the image.

Colour the image according to the code:

Green

Brown

Yellow

Orange

Match the objects to their names.

Zebra

Ostrich

Alarm Clock

Yacht

Dragon

Match the girls with their shadows.

Write the missing letters to complete the names of the objects.

C_T

B _ A _

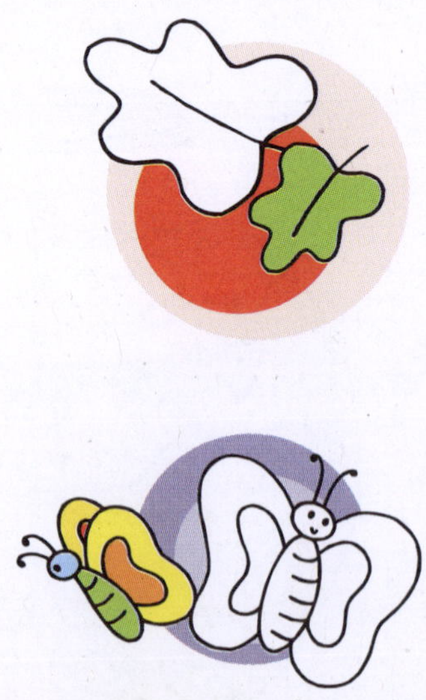

Find the bigger one in each pair and colour it the same as the smaller one.

Look at the images and write their names in the blank.

Colour the picture to make Tina look prettier.

Complete the pattern and colour too.

Match the images with their shadows.

Trace the path to help the S reach the monkey

Count all the balloons and write the number in the square.

There are ☐ balloons.

Calculate and write the number of tigers.

Connect the dots to complete the picture, then colour it.

Draw the other half of the toy and colour.

Help the grasshopper find his way through the maze to the lush green grass.

Count how many plants John has.

In pots:

the ground :

Total:

Count and write the number of puppies.

Complete the picture of the doll, and colour it.

Match the images to their correct shadows.

Match each image to the first letter of its name.

Add the objects and write the number in the square.

Count the dots on each ladybug. Draw a line to join the ladybugs with the same number of dots.

Oliver and emily are playing a dice game. Help them find the answer by adding 1 to each of the dice.

Write the first letter of each animal.

Colour the genie the same way as the reference picture.

Count the objects on the left and circle the correct number.

Circle the odd one out.

Match the phrase with the correct picture.

I am an amphibian.

I can fly.

I live in the water.

I am the king of the jungle.

I love flowers.

Delete the letter "B" from the grid to discover what Mark wants to be when he grows up.

F I B R E B M A B N

Colour the ladder in red.

Circle the objects that belong to a firefighter.

Circle the largest object in each group.

Help Aladdin find the path that will lead him to the magic lamp.

Hold this page in front of a mirror to reveal the characters.

Match the birds with their correct beaks. Write the corresponding numbers in the circles.

Connect the dots from 1 to 35 and colour the image with your favourite colours.

Count how many colourful parrots you can see here.

Fill the blanks with numbers to find the right gate number.

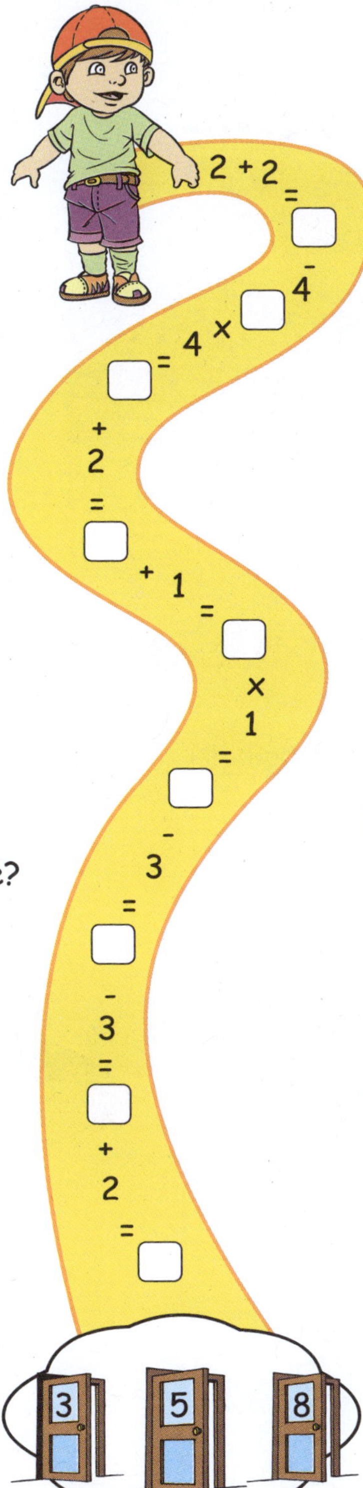

Follow the multiples of 5 to help the rabbit reach his yummy carrots.

Look closely. Can you count the number of triangles in this picture?

The total number of triangles is:

____

Number the images in the order of their appearance in the story.

Find the identical shapes and color them the same.

Help the astronaut slide down the rocket.

Find 8 differences between the two drawings.
Also, colour the images.

Help the boys reach their belongings by following the strings.

Connect the dots from 1 to 20 and colour the drawing.

Match the clocks that indicate the same time.

Copy the snail in the empty grid. Also, colour as shown.

Complete these sequences and colour them.

In each row, circle the object that is identical to the first.

Fill in the missing letters to name the images, then colour them.

L_AF

Count the number of clouds and birds, and then colour them.

Number of clouds:

Number of birds:

Find at least 6 differences between the two drawings.

Match the objects that belong together.

Fill in the empty apples to complete the number secquence.

Trace the path and help Jack find his way to the castle. Be careful not to get lost in the clouds.

Solve the sums on the fish on the right, and then match them to the fish with the right answers.

Colour the areas to match the dots and reveal the hidden picture.

Draw a line to match the candles that are identical.

Match the animal to its favorite food by writing its number in the circle.

Mathew hung a few clothes upside down by mistake. Color only the clothes that are hung correctly.

Fill in the missing letters to complete the words on the left. Then match them to the word that sounds the same.

Complete the drawing.

Trace the path of the bee to her hive.

Circle the first letter of the name of the object.

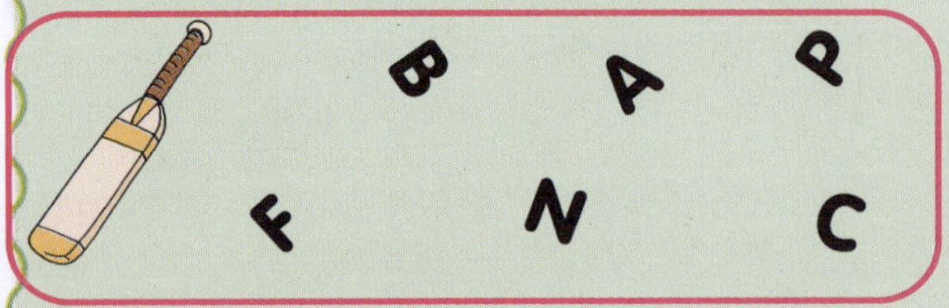

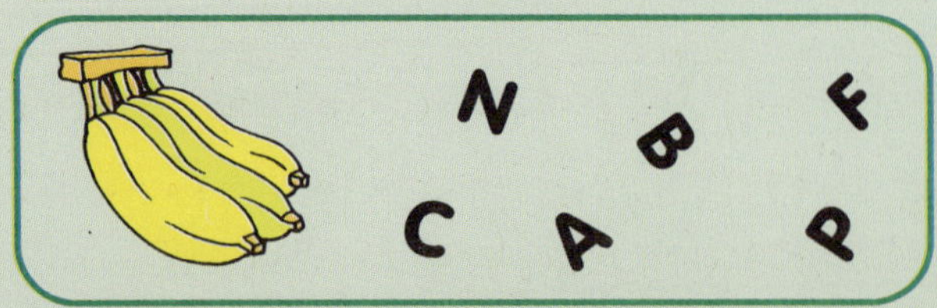

Join the dots to complete the picture and colour it.

Count the stars on the clown's clothes and write down the number.

Help Jessica find her way through maze to reach the chocolate.

Count the number of small and big spots on the frog's body.

Small spots: Big spots Total

Circle the correct name of the object.

Can you help the frog get to its food? Watch out for predators!

Count the number of shapes in each picture below. Write them down and colour the pictures.

______ Square
______ Triangles

______ Rectangles
______ Circles
______ Square
______ Triangles

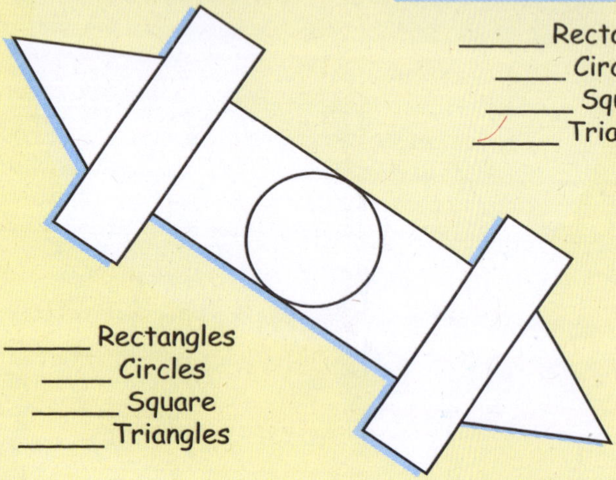

______ Rectangles
______ Circles
______ Square
______ Triangles

Count the number of beads you see in this necklace.

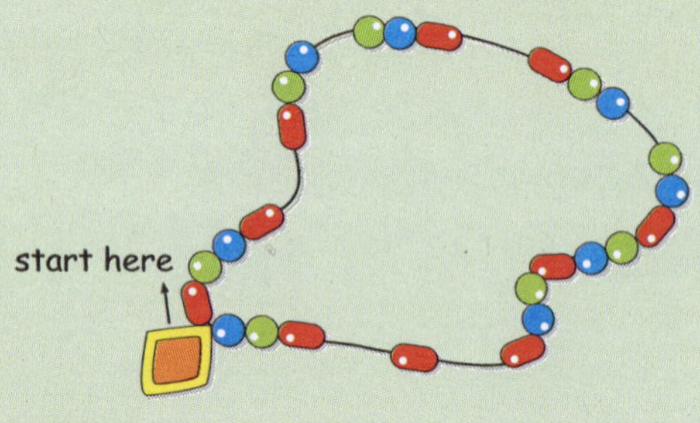

Find and circle 8 differences between these two drawings.

Match the objects that go together.

Connect the dots to reveal the picture, then colour it.

Help Sophie to match her socks. Also, colour them in pairs.

Connect the dots from 1 to 25 and colour the drawing.

Number these drawings in the order of their appearance in the story and colour the drawings.

Trace the path to help the rocket reach its planet.

To find the name of Bob's best friend, colour the letters hidden in the puzzle.

The name of the best friend of bob is:

Colour the butterfly using the colour code given below.

1 blue 2 green 3 red 4 orange 5 yellow

Join the dots to discover the character, and colour it.

Identify the sequences of numbers and complete them.

Match the objects that go together.

Circle the first letter of the name of the object.

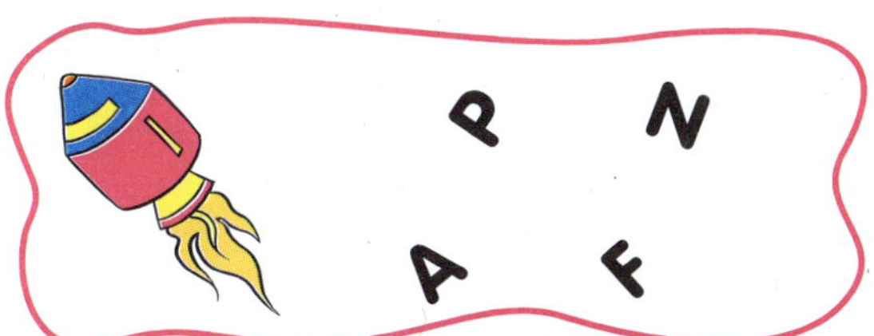

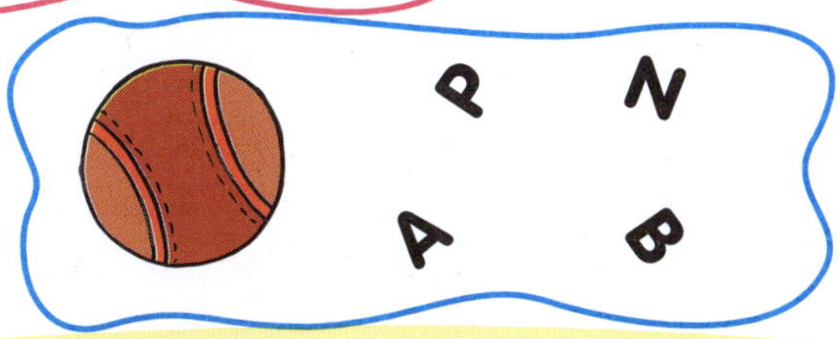

Circle the correct name of the object.

Help the farmer get to his cow.

Draw the picture below to match the one above, then colour it.

Colour the shapes according to the given code.

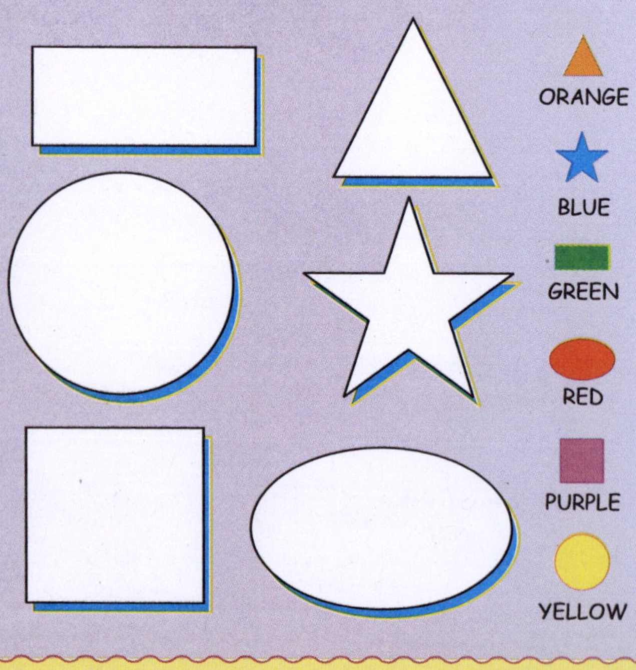

Count the number of objects in each set and match it to the correct number.

In each row, circle the animal that is looking in a different direction.

Colour the animals that can swim in blue and the ones that can fly in green.

Connect the numbers from 1 to 15 to complete the picture, then colour it.

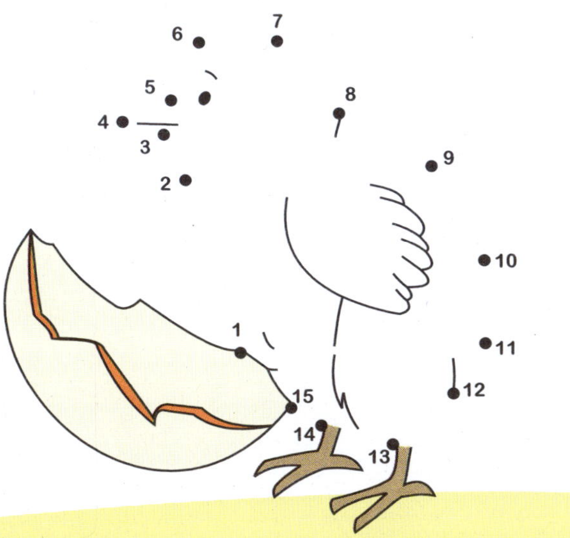

Draw a line to match each sail with the sailboat it belongs to. Then have fun drawing patterns on the hulls of the sailboats.

Join the dots and complete the picture.

Count the objects in each jar and write the amount found in the rectangle.

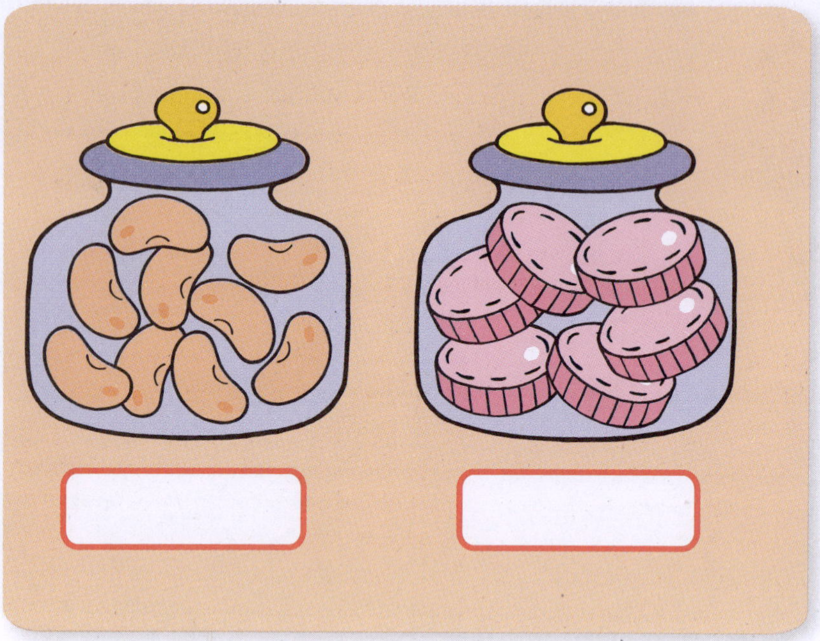

Unscramble the letters to form the right words.

Place the images in order to form a story and then colour the pictures.

Help our little robot find his rocket.

Complete the picture and colour the jewels in the treasure chest.

Help Isha match each pillow to the right bed.

Complete the following words.

U_B_E_L_

R_B_I_

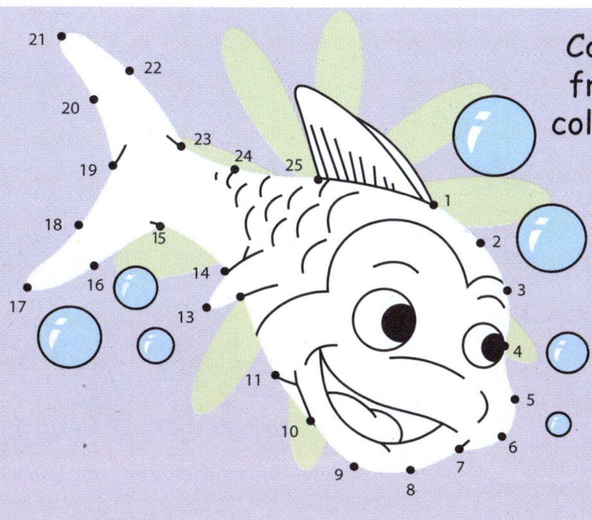

Connect the dots from 1 to 25 and colour the drawing.

Colour the shapes as shown on the left.

Copy each picture and colour it.

How many circles can you see in the picture? Count them and write the number in the box.

Help Samay reach his boat to go fishing.

Look at the fruit bowl picture above. Trace the same picture below and colour it.

connect the dots with even numbers from 2 to 90 and colour the drawing.

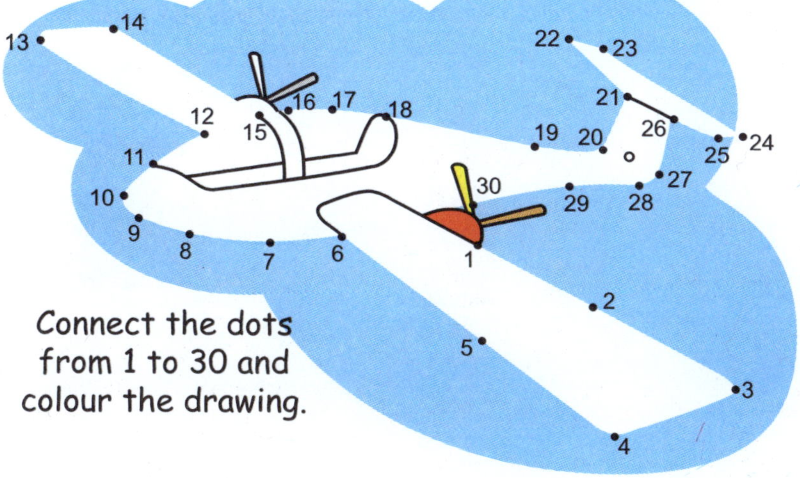

Connect the dots from 1 to 30 and colour the drawing.

Look at the pictures below, then find their names in the grid.

F	I	S	H	L	L	O	O	E	E
T	T	N	N	D	M	D	J	J	A
A	S	S	F	L	O	W	E	R	L
L	W	W	I	I	N	H	C	A	R
S	C	U	P	T	I	H	A	P	F
O	R	D	I	N	T	T	A	P	F
N	B	U	T	T	E	R	F	L	Y
X	R	H	E	K	R	S	M	E	X

Fill the grid so that the numbers 1, 2, 3 and 4 appear in each vertical coloumn, and each horizontal row. No number can appear twice in a row or coloumn.

3		4	
1			
	1		4
	3		2

Match the opposites.

long

small

new

thin

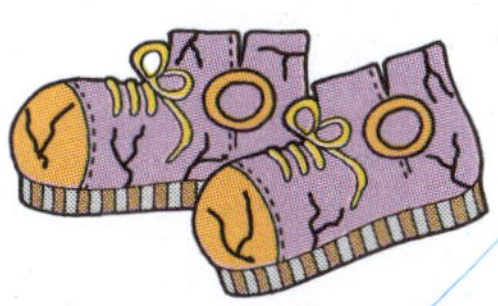

old

thick

big

short

Count and write the number of each different object.

Complete each word with the letters in the clouds.

Bablu has many things in his house. Circle the objects that begin with the letter C.

Count the objects in each jar and write the number in the rectangle.

Connect the dots from 1 to 15 and colour the drawing.

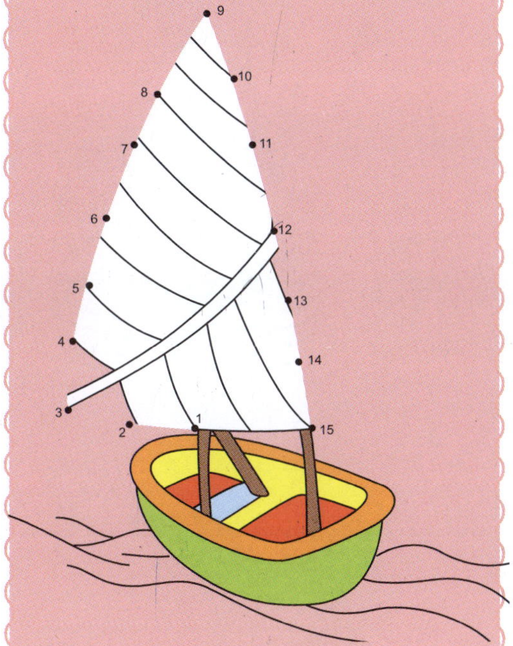

Connect the dots to finish the drawing.

Who am I?

D_ _K

Solve the sums and write the answer in the correct box.

Circle all the objects that come in pairs.

How many squares are there in each box? Calculate the total number of squares and write it in the empty box..

Circle the odd object in each row.

Complete the picture so that both cakes look the same.

Place the book upside down in front of a mirror to see the names of the characters.

Solve the sums and write the answers.

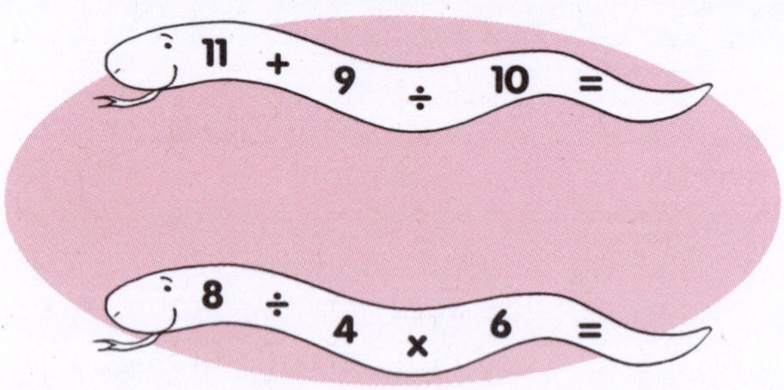

Colour the spaces with dots in pink and the rest in green to find out who is hiding in the picture. How many of them can you see?

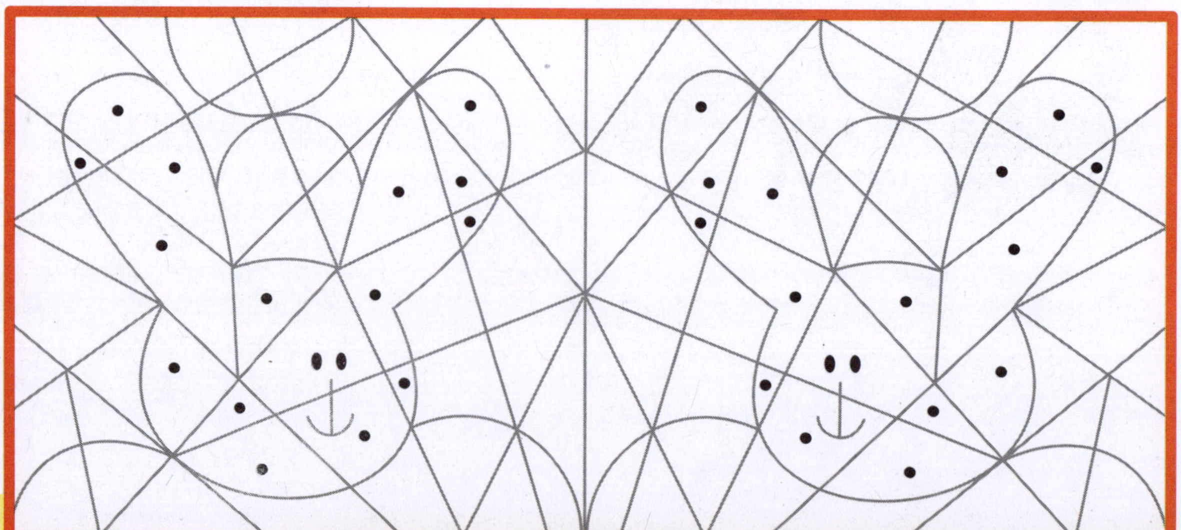

Connect the dots from 1 to 20 and colour the picture.

Copy each picture and colour it in.

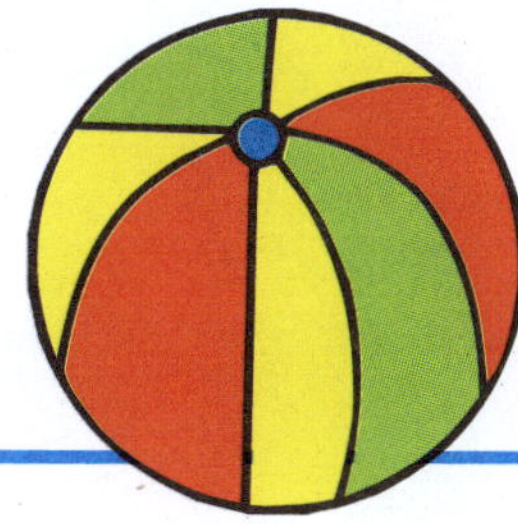

Find around 8 and differences between the two images.

Each child in Column A is missing something. Find the missing item in Column B and draw a line to match it with the correct child.

Colour the animals and draw a line between each animal and its shadow in the opposite column.

Name each object below and connect it to the letter it starts with.

Solve the sums and help the girl reach her dress.

Copy this picture onto the empty grid.

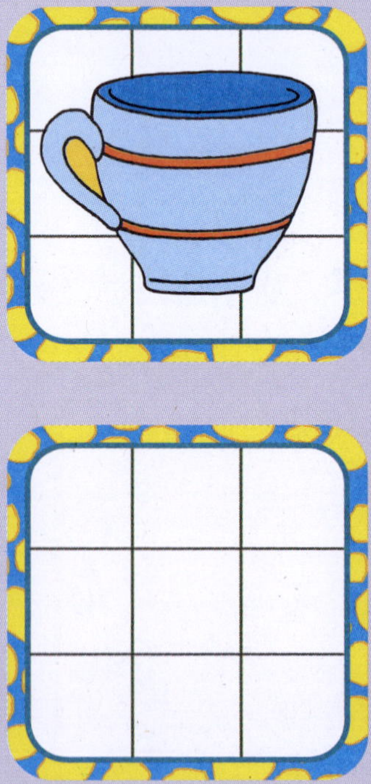

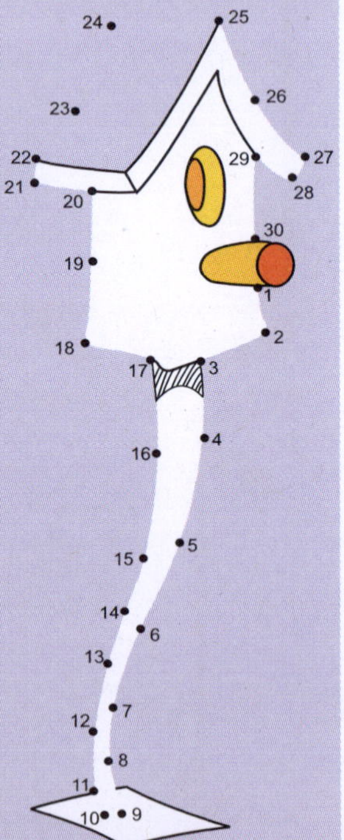

Connect the dots from 1 to 30 and colour the drawing.

3	4		
			1
2		4	
1			4

2			4
	4	2	
	3		
1			3

Fill the grid so that the numbers 1, 2, 3 and 4 appear in each vertical line in each horizontal line. No number can appear twice in a row.

Help the bee reach the flower.

Write as many words as possible inside the mushrooms following the indications.

How many different items do you see on the set? Count them and colour them.

Two of these puppies are twins. Connect them.

Connect the dots from 1 to 25 and then color the whole picture.

Solve the sums and write the answers.

15 ÷ 3 × 7 =

9 - 6 + 8 =

13 - 3 ÷ 5 =

Colour the piece that is missing from the vase.

Colour the similar shapes in same colour.

Find around 6 and differences between the two images, then colour them.

Help the juggler find his juggling balls.

Fill in the missing numbers to complete the sequence.

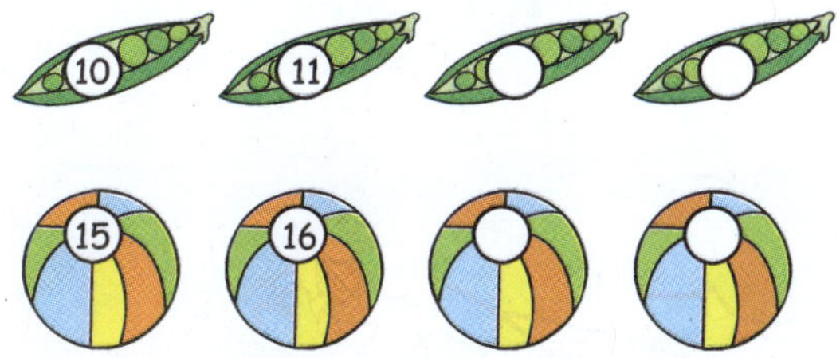

Count the total number of objects in each set and write the answers.

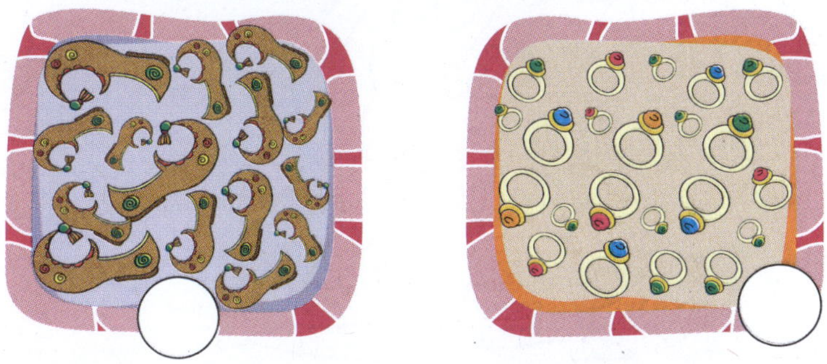

Combine the belts to the correct dresses.

Find the following shapes in the drawing and then colour them.

Trace and complete the picture to make it look the same as the one in the right.

The electrician must match the lamps with their sockets. Help him by drawing a line between the lamp and the socket, then drawing patterns on the lampshade.

Write the missing numbers on the leaves.

Complete the patterns on the flag and colour them.

Circle the pair that is the smallest in this group.

Connect the dots from 1 to 25 and colour the drawing.

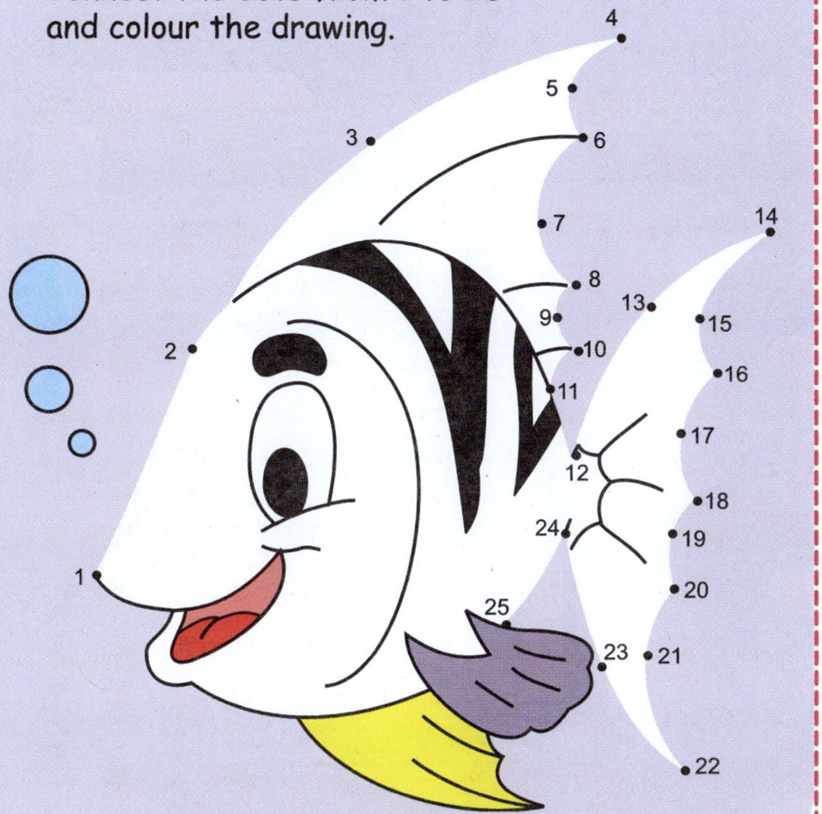

Draw some more marbles in each bag until there are 10 marbles in every bag.

Match the dice (or pair of dice) to the number they show.

trace the lines to find out which bracelet belongs to Anu, Rama, Riya and Mina.

Help the magician reach his hat.

Find 5 differences between the two images.

Help Abhi find the mummy.

Write as many words as possible in each mushroom following the indications.

Name and colour the tools Jaya will need for gardening.

Count the total number of objects in each set and write the answers.

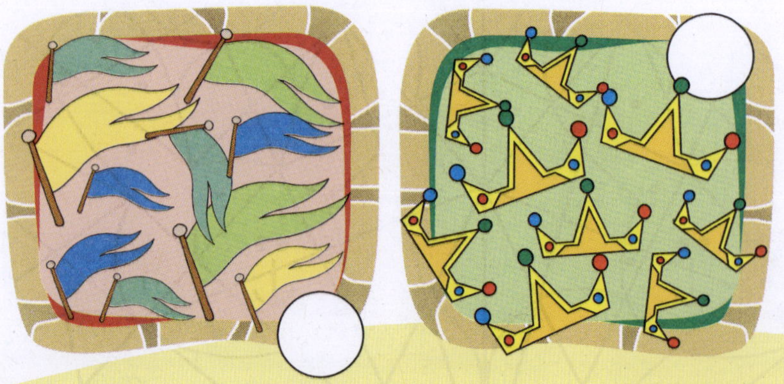

Circle the larger object in each group.

Count the number of balls in each bag and write the number.

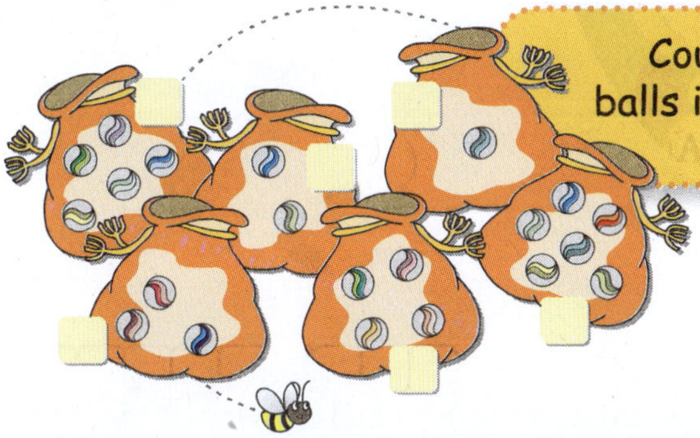

Connect the dots from 1 to 15 and colour the drawing.

Trace the path that leads Jai to the pink flag.

How many trees did he cross?

Write a sentence to describe the scene in the image, then colour it..

Look at the pattern carefully and complete the sequence.

Fill in the lemons with multiples of 3.

Help the bird find its nest so it can feed its young.

Follow the number code to colour the picture.

1 blue, 2 green, 3 red, 4 orange, 5 yellow

Trace the path and help Martin reach the flag.

Can you make the second picture look like the first? Draw what's missing and colour it.

Circle the odd one in each row.

Connect the dots from 1 to 25 and colour the drawing.

Join the dots and colour the picture.

Circle the odd one in each row.

Colour the smaller animal in each pair.

Connect the even-numbered dots from 2 to 60 and colour the picture.

Circle the odd one out in each group.

Follow the correct string to help Dev get to his pizza.

Help the sparrow reach its food.

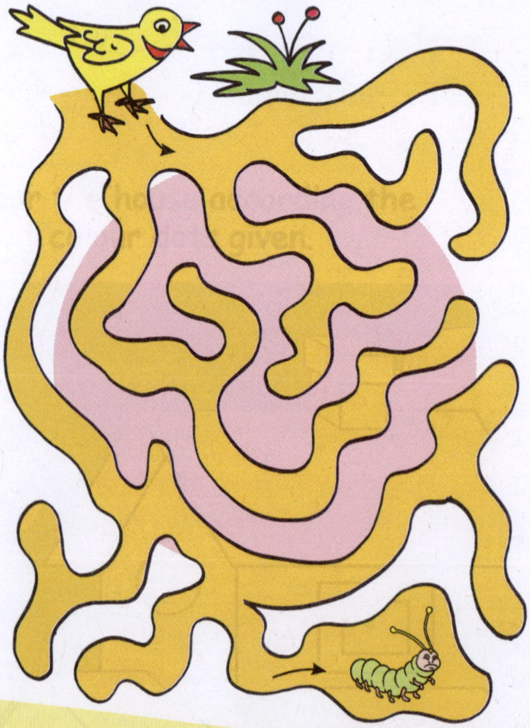

Colour the shirts with 5 buttons: red, 3 buttons: yellow, 4 buttons: green, and 6 buttons: blue.

Connect the shapes with their correct names.

Count the number of objects in each set and write the answers.

Connect the similar-looking leaves, and colour them in the same colour.

Join the dots in order to find the mystery animal and write its name.

Complete the names of Jay's favourite toys by filling in the blanks.

Colour the pairs of similar-looking shapes the same colour.

Connect the rabbits in the correct order, starting from 1 to 10.

Help the butterfly land on the flower.

Help Peter find his ice cream before it melts.

Draw and colour 5 rabbits in the garden.

Connect the dice to the numbers they show.

Count the number of sides each shape has and write the answer in the circle.

In each row, read the number written on the left and colour the same number of objects. Also, write the number.

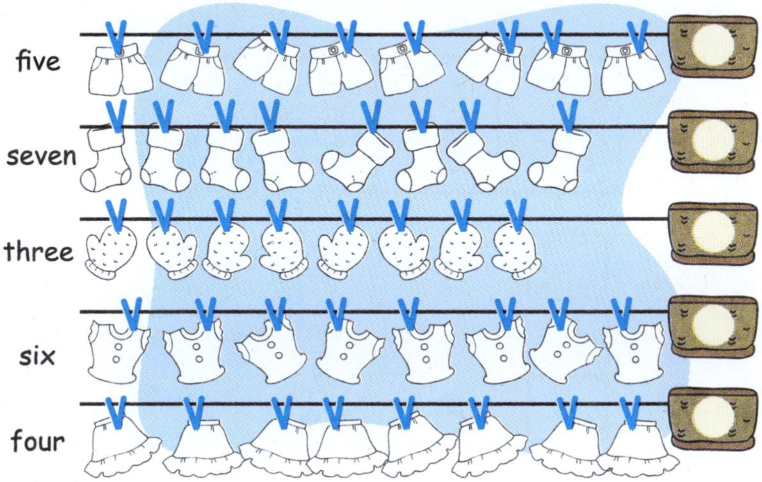

Connect the dots from 1 to 25 to see who caught the fish, and then colour the picture.

Say the numbers written below out loud.

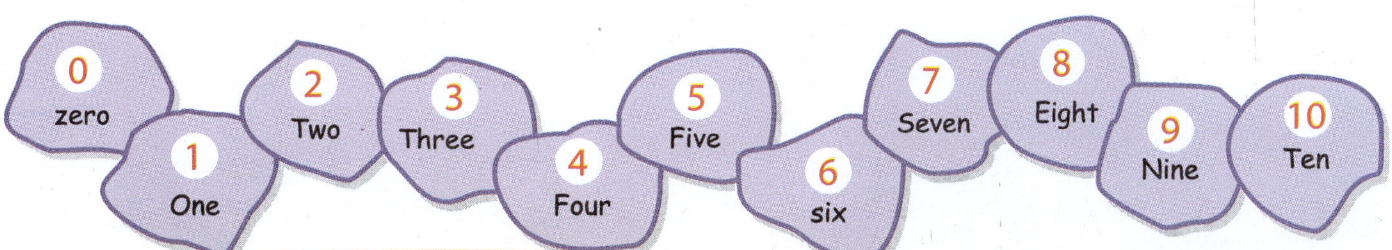

Count the number of hearts in each set.

Total

Help the ant reach the sugar cubes.

Can you turn these ovals into a crab and a fish? Draw what's missing.

Write an even number on each luggage trolley and colour them.

Circle the smallest item in each group and colour the big one.

Draw an even number of flowers in each patch and write the number. Then, trace the bee's path.

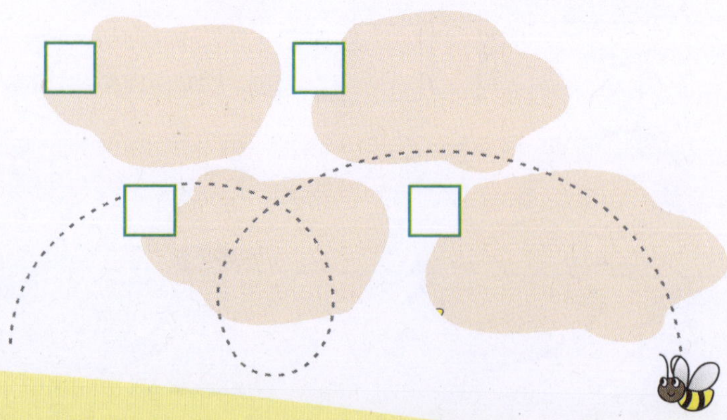

Count the number of objects in each set and write it in the box.

Connect numbers on the icecream to their number names.

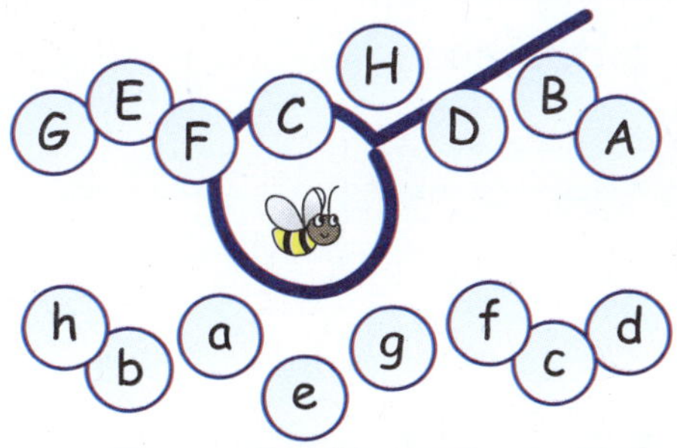

Connect the upper case letters to their correct lower case letters.

Connect the dots from 1 to 20 and colour the drawing.

There are four-sided shapes on the beach. Tick the shapes that would form the windows of the castle. Also, colour.

Cross the heavier object by looking at the balance.

Circle the largest object in each group.

Write the missing numbers and their names.

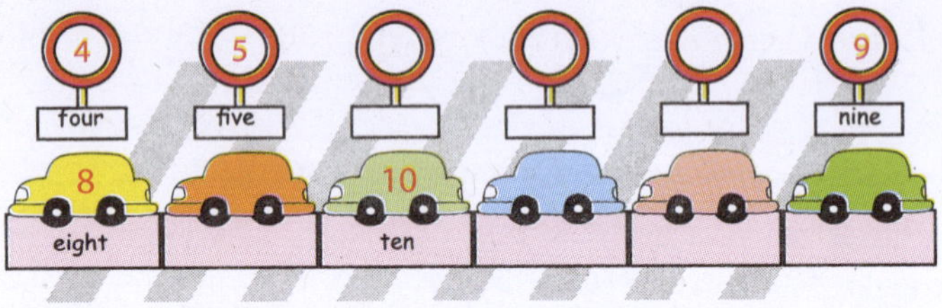

Colour the robot by following the colour code.

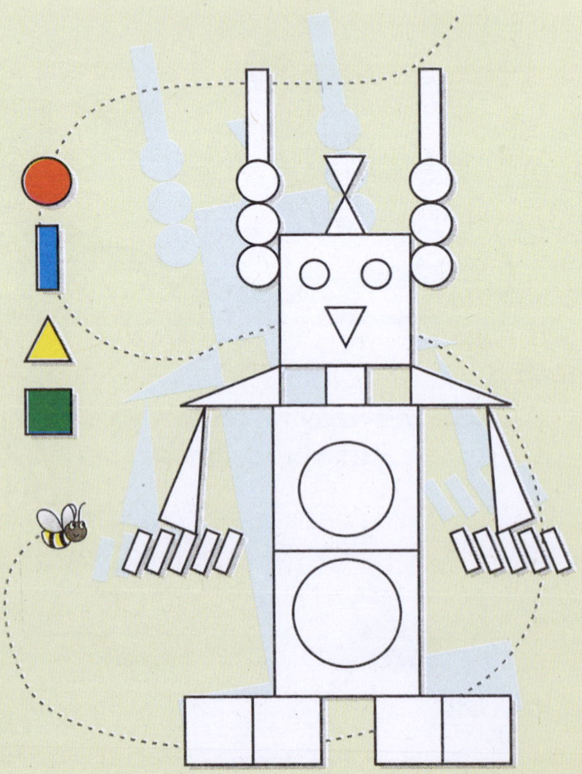

Look at the example to find objects that belong together. Colour each group with its own colour.

Trace the path to help Manu reach home.

Count the number of 🌷 in each group. Write the answer in figure and in word.

Count the items and write the number. Circle the group that has more.

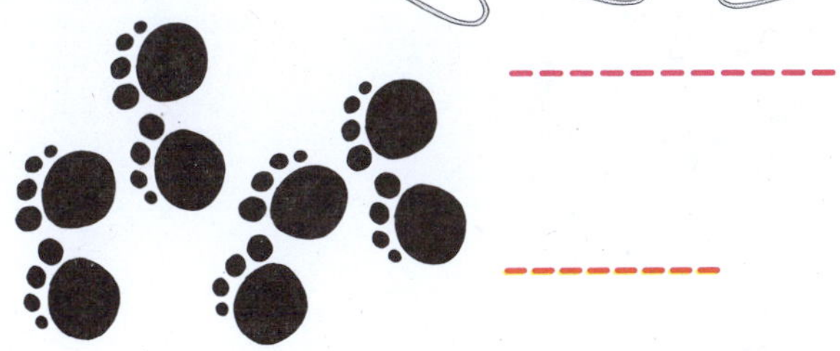

Find the correct missing piece of the broken mirror

Count the objects on the farm and write the correct number.

Colour the drawing.

Connect the dots from 1 to 25 and colour the drawing.

Connect the dots from 1 to 25 and colour drawing.

Connect the dots from 1 to 25 and colour drawing.

Draw a line from each bear to the football with a bigger number.

Colour all the smileys with a number greater than 10 in yellow and those with numbers less than 10 in green.

Trace the path to help Kiran reach the icecream.

Identify the different body parts as indicated and join the circled letters in the correct order to find the secret word.

The secret word is:

_ _ _ _ _

How many squares can you find in the box on the left?

in all   in all

Add the number of objects in each group and write the answers.

Help the snake slither its way into the forest.

Circle the leaves the beetle ate, starting from 1. Then, write the numbers of the leftover leaves below.

Colour the plates that contain more than three objects.

Help the red candle find its way to the birthday cake.

Complete the pictures by adding the missing elements.

Match the blackboards that have the same number of objects. Also, draw the number of objects on the whiteboard as stated.

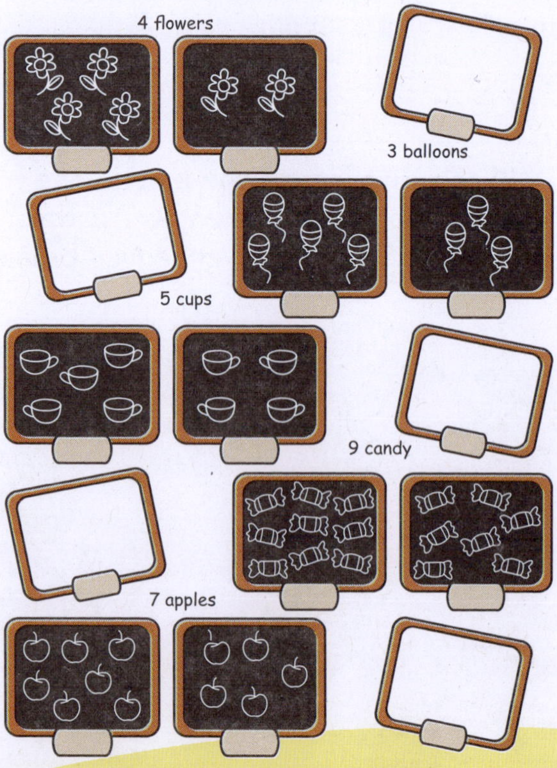

Follow the color code to discover which number is hiding in the picture.

Code:

a - black	b - orange	C - rose
d - red	e - yellow	z - blue

The hidden number is: ________

Trace the path to help Mathew fetch his umbrella.

Add the numbers on the Tortoises and write the answer.

Help Sai unlock the rooms. Draw a line from each key to its matching door.

Draw the same image as shown in the empty grid.

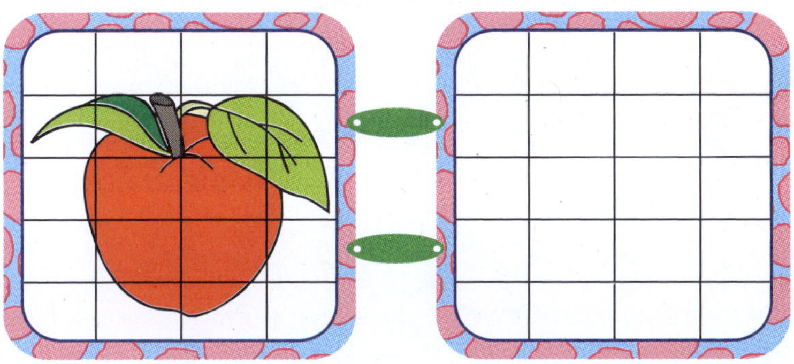

Count the number of objects in each set and write it in the box

Fill in the missing numbers by adding 5 each time.

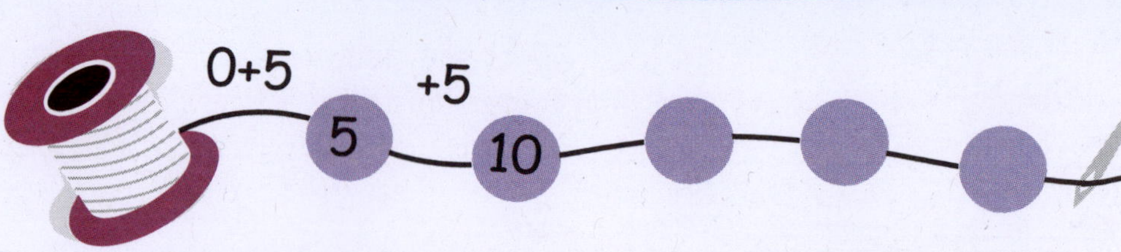

Fill in the blanks to complete the words. Look at the objects below for clues.

Connect the dots and name the animal.

Identify 8 differences between the two pictures. Also, colour.

Can you copy the fish from the aquarium? Draw it and color it in.

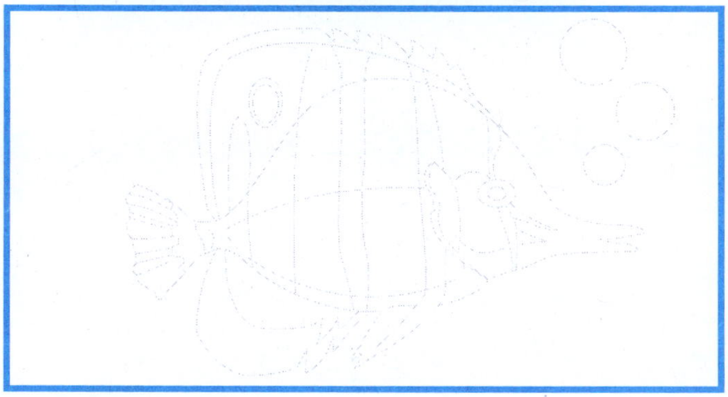

Help the squirrel collect the nuts.

Count how many of each object you see and write the number. Colour the pictures the same colour as shown below.

How often these drawings appear?

In each box indicates the number of times each object appears.

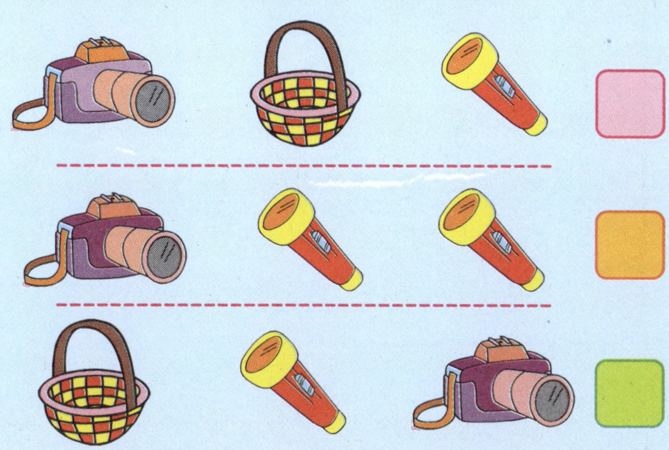

Write the names of the animals below.

Help the chicken join its chick.

Solve these problems and write the answers.

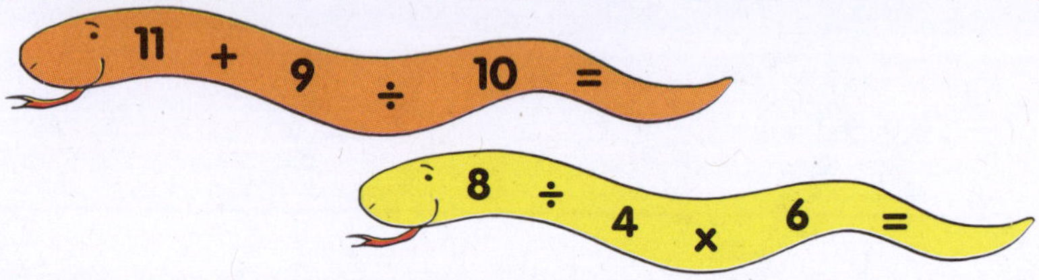

Use the number code to color the spaces and see what the image is.

What is it? ... .

Mark the things we use to tell time.

Can you help the mouse find the cheese? The right path is the result, which is 30.

Connect the characters with their names.

Aladdin

Princess

Sultan

Magician

Genie

Count and write the number of red squares each set has.

Can you find the name of each animal by their body parts?

How many of each item can you find? Count them and write it down.

Write the numbers in descending order starting with the highest number.

How many cubes are there in each set?

__ tens + __ units = __

__ tens + __ units = __

__ tens + __ units = __

Count the number of red squares in each set.

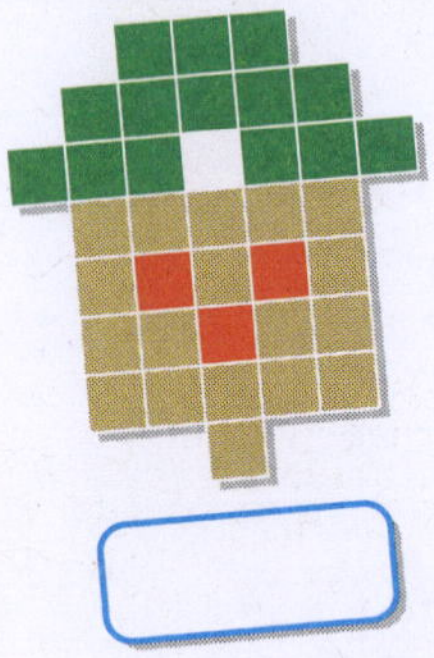

Use the code given below to find the solution!

Where has the mother of Jacques sent him to sell the cow?

Help Mr. grasshopper reach the leaf.

Circle the odd one out in each group.

Connect the dots from 1 to 25 to find out who is getting ready to jump into the water and then colour the picture.

Write the missing numbers.

Count and write the number of times each different shape appears in the picture.

Circle the largest object in each group.

Write the missing numbers by adding 4 at each step.

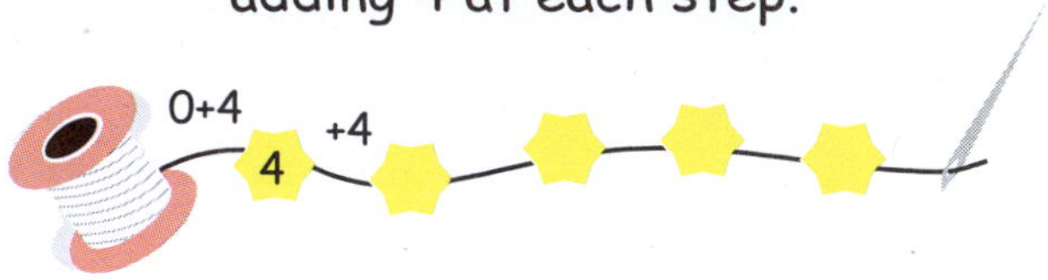

Draw lines to give the even kites to Mary and the odd kites to Peter.

Draw and colour 16 stars, 8 carpets and 4 magic lamps in the given space.

Help the mummy return to its grave.

Circle the first element in each row.

Colour the pictures that are different from those in the squares.

Solve these sums to find the way to the garden. The right path is the result of which is 4.

Connect the dots from 1 to 15 to find out what the boy has in his hand and then colour the picture.

Trace the path to help the mouse come to the ground.

Use the fruit code to find the numbers and solve these sums.

Trace the path between the bird and fish.

Connect the dots and colour the picture.

Circle the correct missing piece of the broken mirror.

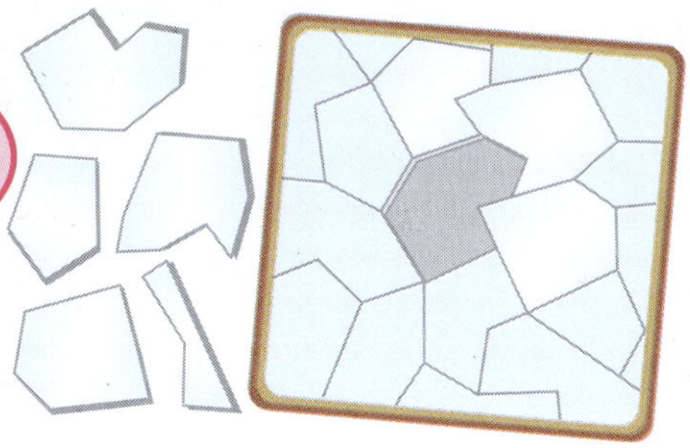

Write a sentence to describe what is happening in the picture and colour it.

Match the similar-looking cars and colour them.

Colour the animals in the food chain.

Trace the path to help Aladdin find the princess.

Trace the path to help Karan reach his home.

Colour the picture using the example below.

Draw and colour the other half of the butterfly as shown.

Circle all the toys and objects you can play with.

How many balls and balloons have you found? ________

How many bats have you found? ________

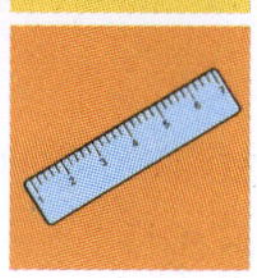

Count and write the number of animals shown in each set.

Connect each cup to the saucer with the same number. Colour each set with the same colour.

Can you identify each animal by looking at their body parts?

Colour the lion.

Connect the dots from 1 to 25 and colour the drawing.

Match the similar-looking camels.

Which of these kites belong to Rohan?

Help Annie reach her gift.

Help the robot draw a line between the rockets in the order of the days of the week.

Add the numbers on the snails and write their sums.

Connect each bear to the football whose number is higher than his.

Write the days of the week on the boats, starting with Monday.

In each row, circle the animal that does not look in the same direction as the others.

Match the numbers to the group with the same number of objects.

Match the word with the right image.

SCIENTIST DOCTOR

CARPENTER NURSE CLEANER

Circle all the jungle animals in the table below.

Circle the first letter of the object.

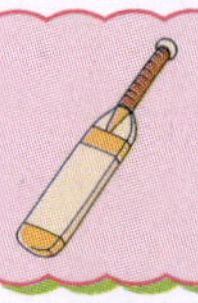

B A P F N C

N B F C A P

P N C A F R B

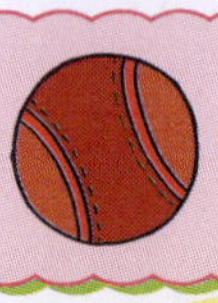

P N C A B R

Circle the objects that begin with the letter T.

Connect the numbers 1 to 30 to discover the hidden picture.

Colour the image.

Help the mouse reach the cheese by drawing a line through the maze.

Name the objects and colour them as shown.

Write the missing numbers in the balloons.

Connect the dots and colour Anne's dress.

How many faces do you see in this picture?

I counted ____________ faces.

Unscramble the letters and write the words. The answers are written on the carpet.

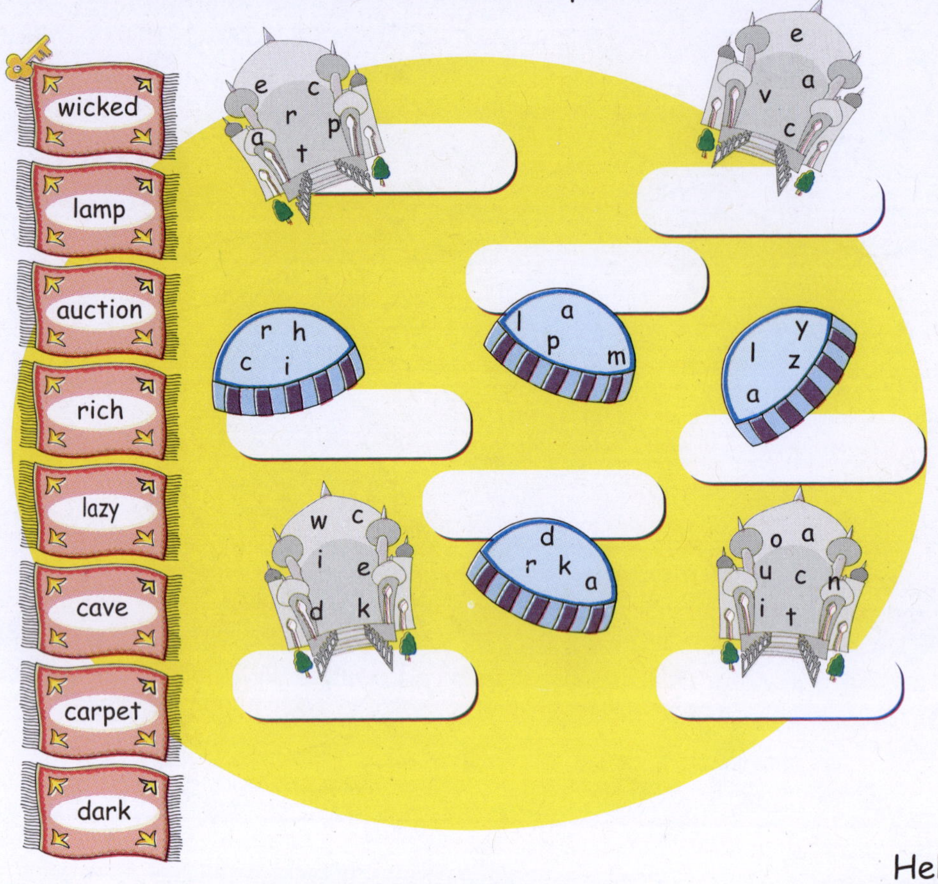

Help Jack find his way home.

Write the missing numbers by adding 3 each time.

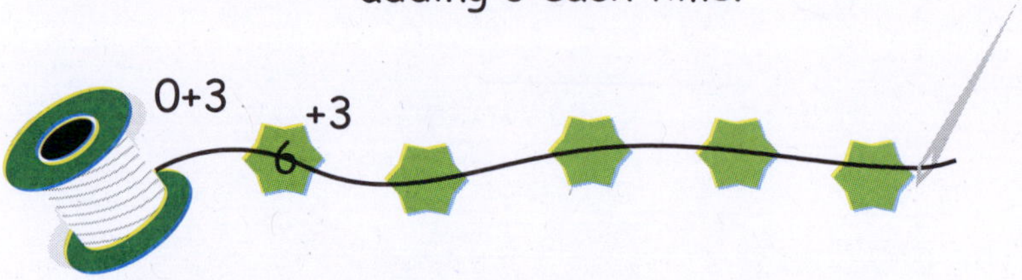

Help Tom to add new fish in his aquarium.

add 2 6 and 7 .

Circle the plates that have more than three fruits.

Multiply and then trace a line along the multiples of 3. This path will lead you to the secret room.

3 × 1 =	2 × 2 =	7 × 2 =	1 × 11 =
4 × 4 =	3 × 2 =	5 × 0 =	4 × 4 =
3 × 3 =	5 × 3 =	6 × 1 =	4 × 3 =
5 × 4 =	5 × 2 =	3 × 5 =	2 × 10 =
1 × 13 =	8 × 1 =	3 × 6 =	4 × 2 =
4 × 5 =	2 × 8 =	3 × 7 =	3 × 4 =

Look at the pictures and help Kavya name these objects. Then colour them.

Colour the dotted sections to discover Jeet's favorite toy.

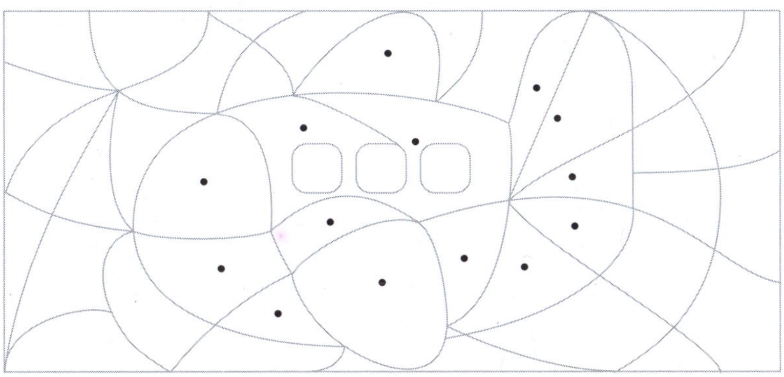

Help the dog reach his bone.

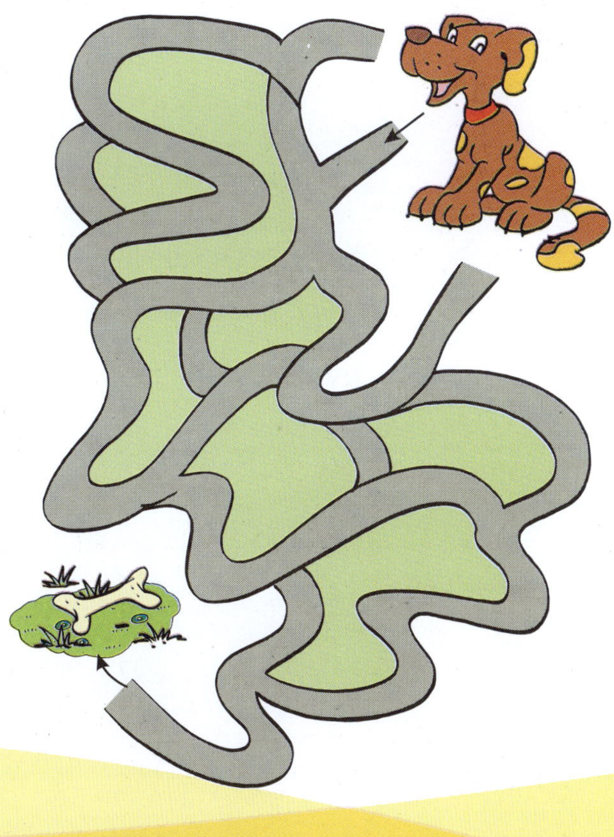

Connect these girls to their favourite dolls.

Colour all the tools John need for gardening.

Connect the even numbered dots from 2 to 80 and color the picture.

Write the names of the objects. you see below.

Write the missing numbers counting by adding 8 at each step.

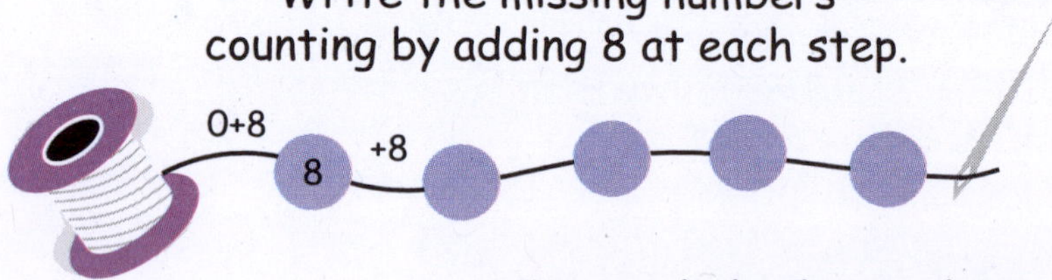

Can you help the monkey to get to his favourite bananas?

Colour the dotted sections in pink and the rest green to find the hidden image. Whose image is it?

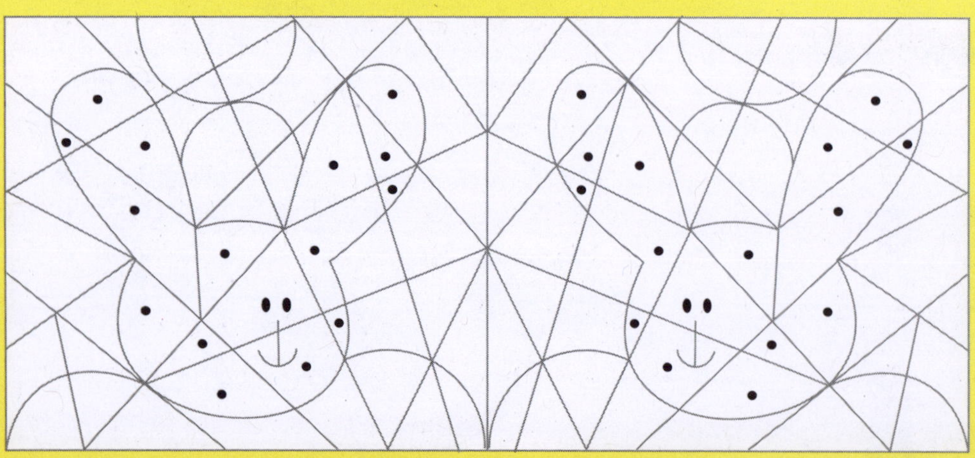

Colour the cards bearing vowels. Put the letters in order to find the object that Mohan uses to talk to his friends.

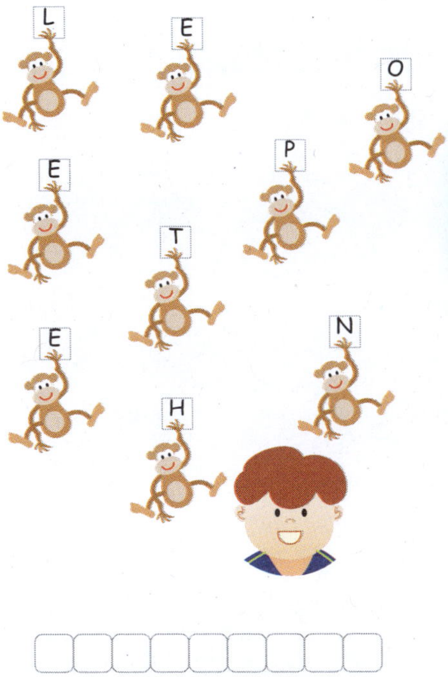

Connect the object and the bee that has the same letter.

Connect the dots from 1 to 25 and colour the drawing.

Cross out all the letter 'B's to see what Ravi wants to be when he grows up.

Colour the ladder in red.

Circle the objects that belong to the firefighter.

Help the bird get inside the wooden birdhouse.

Trace the string from each boy to his kite, then colour the kite to match the boy's clothes.

Guide Hari through the trail to reach his bat and ball.

Connect the dots from 1 to 30 and color the drawing.

Draw a line from each boy to his matching kangaroo friend.

Connect the dots from 1 to 35 and colour the drawing.

Helps the nurse reach the stretcher.

Write the counting from 1 to 10.

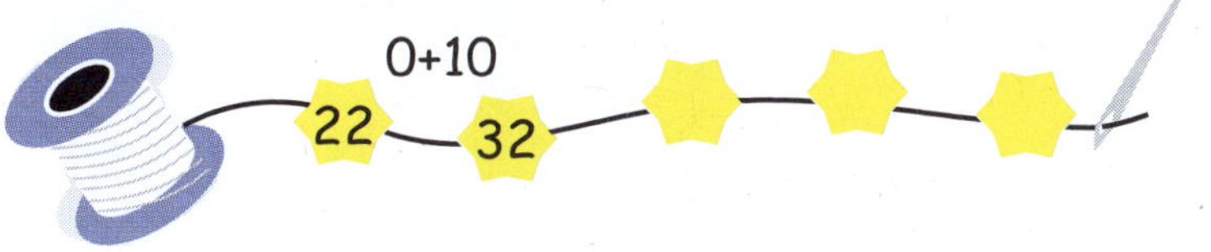

Look at the number grid above and fill in the missing numbers on the bricks.

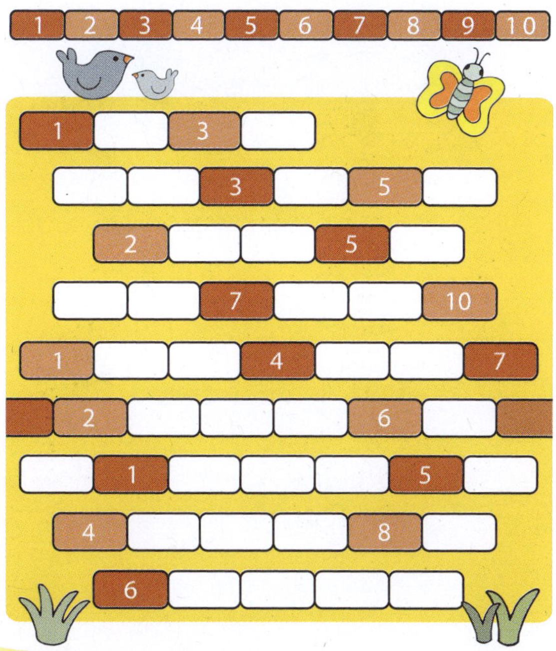

Help Peter unscramble the letters on each pencil to form a word.

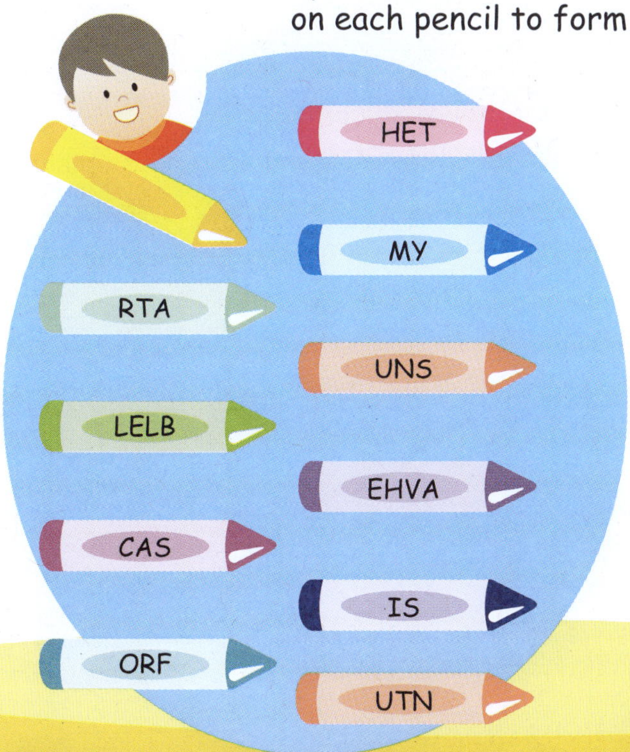

Connect the dots from 1 to 60 and colour the drawing.

Help the skier reach the flag.

Count the clothes on each stand and write the total on the label.

Colour the bears that look to the left in brown and those who look right in black.

Colour the house according the colour dots given.

Draw a line from each fish to the month that has the same number of days

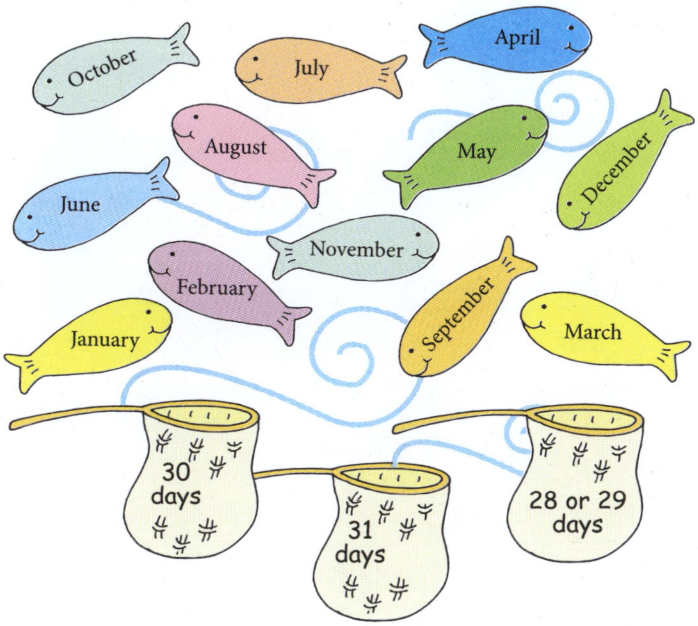

Write the names of the missing months:

January, ----------------, ----------------, April
------------, June, ------------------, ----------------,
September, ----------------, ------------------, ----------------

Decode to find the name of the sport.

0 = A
1 = B
2 = L
3 = S
4 = E

1 0 3 4 1 0 2 2

Match the characters that correspond to the same story.

Connect the dots from 1 to 35 to reveal the picture and then colour.

Help Arun get out of the jungle.

Connect the dots with even numbers from 2 to 90 to discover who is hiding around the flowers, and then colour the picture.

Match the rings with same number of hearts.

Help the shark find fish.

Solve the math problems and draw a path through the multiples of 2 to help the cat find the fish.

			2 x 1 =	3 x 1 =
			4 x 1 =	5 x 1 =
		6 x 1 =	5 x 2 =	6 x 3 =
		2 x 2 =	10 x 1 =	6 x 2 =
3 x 5 =	2 x 3 =	5 x 3 =	7 x 1 =	4 x 3 =
2 x 4 =	4 x 4 =	3 x 3 =	1 x 3 =	9 x 1 =
5 x 4 =	2 x 5 =	4 x 4 =	3 x 4 =	1 x 3 =
4 x 2 =	8 x 2 =	2 x 6 =	5 x 4 =	3 x 5 =
0 x 0 =	5 x 5 =	10 x 1 =		
2 x 7 =	3 x 0 =			

Trace the missing parts of Jyoti's toys. Also, colour them.

Connect points 1 to 10 and colour the picture.

Count the objects and connect them to the correct numbers.

Trace the path and help John reach his home.

Follow the picture number code to solve the given sums.

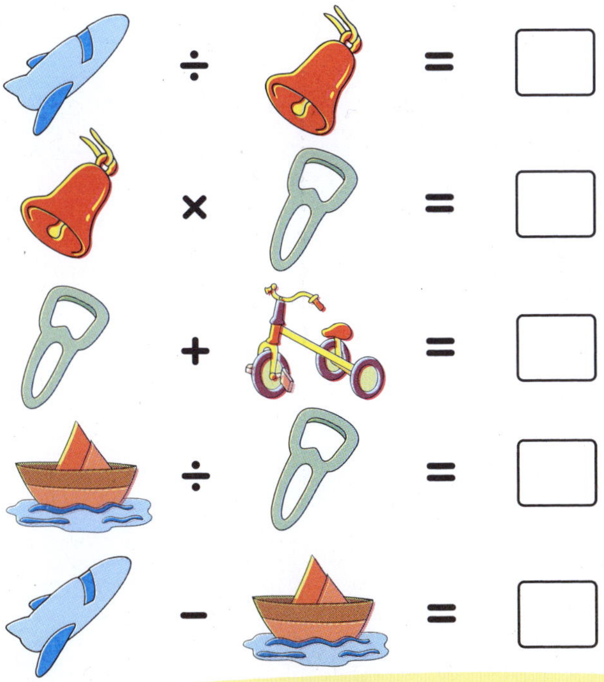

Look at the trees and answer the questions.

How many are there of:

leaves ? ____ = 10 + ____

birds ? ____ = 10 + ____

apples ? ____ = 10 + ____

Trace the path to help the plane land on the ship.

Draw four apples on the tree.
Draw a sun.
Draw three windows on the house.
Draw five balloons in the sky.
Draw two flags at the top of the mountain.
Draw two more clouds.

Connect the dots to complete your friend, Tortie. Then colour her.

Help Mary find her way home. Then colour her home.

It's counting time. Look at the patterns on the umbrella. Count each shape and write the numbers in the circles below.

small spots

big patches

Total

Colour the umbrella.

Help the turtle reach the flag.

Number the images in the correct order.

There are_____________pairs of bears.
There are_____________single bears.

Colour the objects that Sarah needs to go skiing.

Colour as shown in the table below.
The first drawing is done for you.

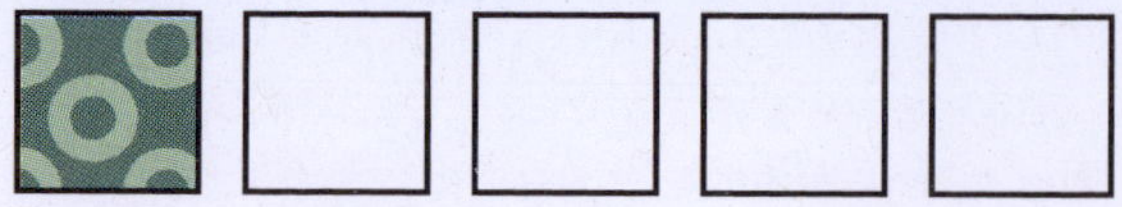

C6 G5 F8 A4 D2

now, colour and : E7, blue - B3, red - F4, orange - H6, black

Name the square that includes the following patterns:

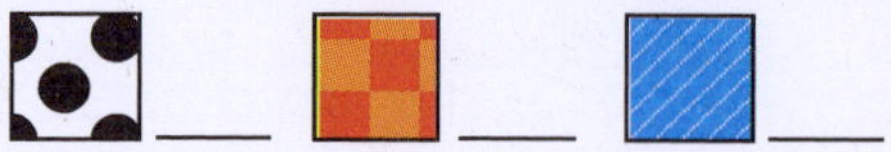

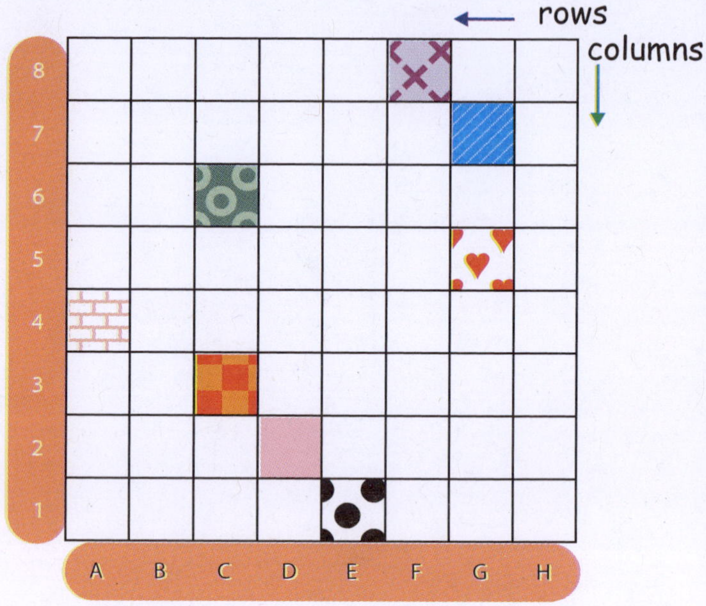

Neha has a collection of bow ties. Count how many are there.

Connect the characters that belong to the same story.

Help the starfish reach the ocean floor.

Trace the lines to see what Marc's father bought him from the mall.

Colour the boxes in the order of the numbers to help the cat catch the mouse.

Similarly, colour the path leading the monkey to the banana.

Colour the letters hidden in the puzzle to find the name of Joan's best friend.

Joan's best friend is

Draw a line to connect the boys and help them complete their phone call.

Connect the dots from 1 to 30 and color picture.

Colour in this patchwork cushion using the instructions below.

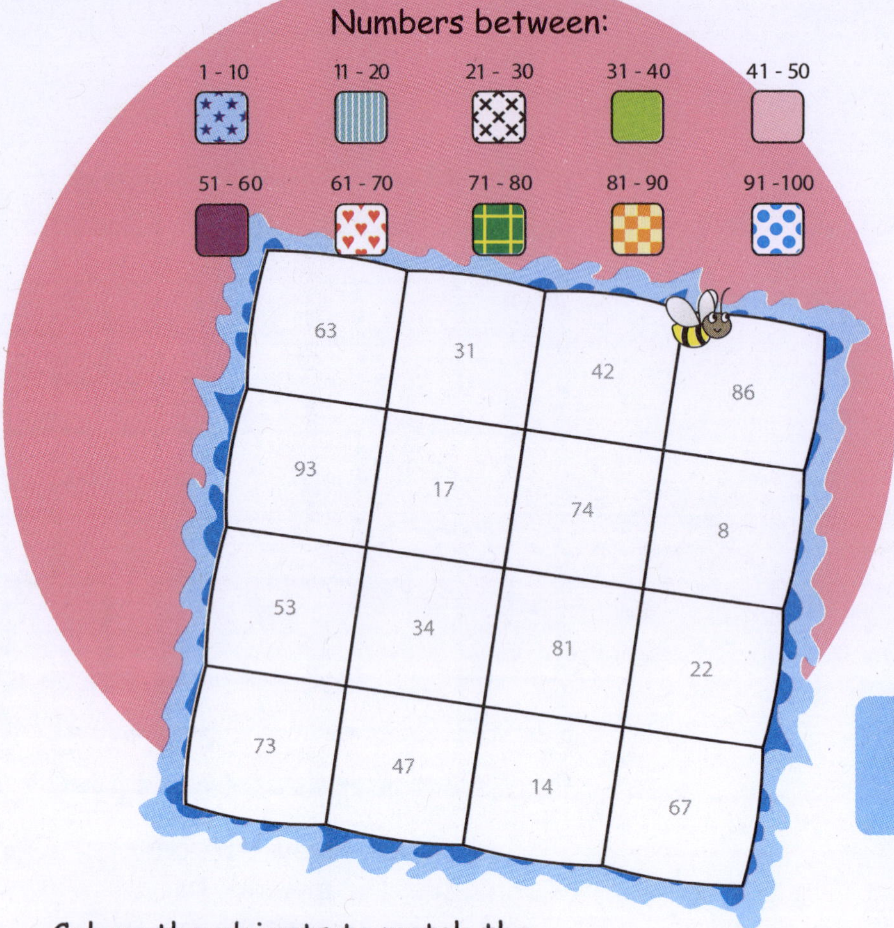

Help the monk find his way to the monastery.

Draw a line from each group of objects to the correct number on the right.

Colour the objects to match the bags so that each bag contains one of each.

Colour Anil's tops with the colour of your choice.

Trace and colour the picture of the dinosaur that John saw in the museum.

Unscramble the letters to discover Anjali's favourite things.

Find the way for the mouse to escape the cat.

Link each number name on the balloon to the correct number on the face of the clown. Colour them.

Colour the dotted space to discover Anu's favourite toy.

The ingredients Cathy needs to bake are placed around. Look at them, and write their names in the given empty circles.

Circle the healthy food.

Paul is walking through the jungle. colour the picture.

Colour the things that Tim, Bob, and Peter saw while returning from a picnic.

Complete the picture and colour it.

Pick a different colour for each item and fill in one square on the graph for every object you count.

Colour the objects you see above.

Colour Nisha's bow ties as per the instructions.

Crack the code to reveal the name of the object.

Help the diver discover the treasure.

Count the number of easter eggs that Mark found and write it in the basket below. Also decorate the eggs.

Jimmy and Tara's clothes look very dull. Colour their clothes in bright colours.

Help the king of the jungle reach the crown.

Help the bird reach her nest.

Follow the dotted lines to see which pizza belongs to Diya. Then, find and colour the oldest and youngest people in her family.

Make as many two-digit numbers as you can from the three numbers below. One has already been done for you.

Write the numbers in increasing order.

72 , ...

....

What numbers have the number 7 in the tens place?

Follow the path in multiples of 5 to help the rabbit reach the carrot.

Help Brownie, the cat find her way through the maze to go fishing.

Jaya has just turned seven. Draw as much candles on her cake.

Help Maya pack her school bag! Find and circle these items in the picture: 1 binder, 3 pencils, 1 bowl, 1 water bottle and 1 box of crayons.

Help Michael find his paintbrushes

How many Easter eggs did Sarah find? Write the number in the basket and add your own designs to the eggs.

Write the missing numbers in each row.

Connect the dots from 1 to 20 and colour drawing.

Read the clues below, choose the matching word from the beans and write it in the crossword grid.

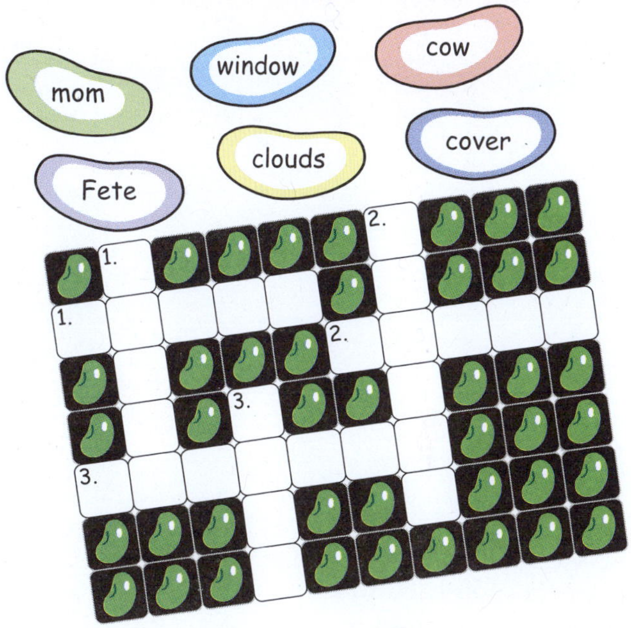

1 horizontal ....

1 vertical ....

2 horizontal ....

2 vertical ....

3 horizontal ....

3 vertical ....

Count the number of objects in each row and circle the correct answer.

Help the caveman return to his cave.

Colour the picture.

Join the dots and colour the drawing.

Connect each object to the butterfly that has its first letter written on it.

Look at the patterns carefully and complete the sequence. Then colour it.

Help the sheep return to her barn.

Help Irfan find his house. It results in the number 7.

In the grid below, write the missing numbers.

7	-		=	4
+		+		+
7	-	5	=	
=		=		=
	-		=	6

Find out the given words from the grid below. Rewrite the words on the coins.

giant

harp

money

hen

boy

Jacques

T	O	N	P	A	E	G	A	S
U	J	A	C	Q	U	E	S	M
E	C	G	A	G	E	A	U	T
U	F	A	R	G	E	N	T	E
H	A	R	P	E	S	T	O	H
W	B	C	R	T	I	G	E	D
A	P	O	U	L	E	L	E	G
D	O	N	T	P	R	O	V	P

Count the number of objects in each row and circle the correct answer.

Colour all the bottles red that form the name of Jacob and blue that form the name of Mary.

Colour the pictures.

Write the names of the animals and circle their young ones.

Fill in the missing numbers by adding 6 at each step.

Connect the dots to complete the picture.

Fill in the missing letter. Also Count the number of flowers, cookies and cups.

Tim has a collection of toy cars. Count them and colour them.

Cross out the smallest number on each instrument and circle the largest.

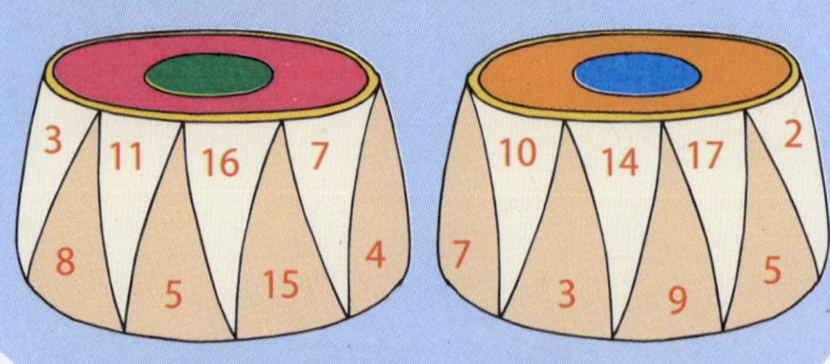

Look at the number on each paint bucket and write the same number on the matching paintbrush.

Connect the dots to complete the image. Then colour it.

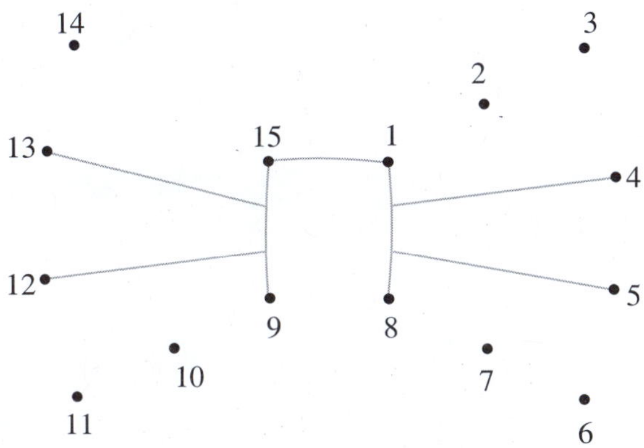

Trace and colour Joel's cool cargo pants.

Help Sanjay get to the center of the balloon.

Connect numbers to the mushrooms with the same number of dots.

Circle all the wild animals.

Count the number of ice creams and connect each box to the right number.

9 8

6 10

Fill in the blanks to complete the words and then colour the drawings.

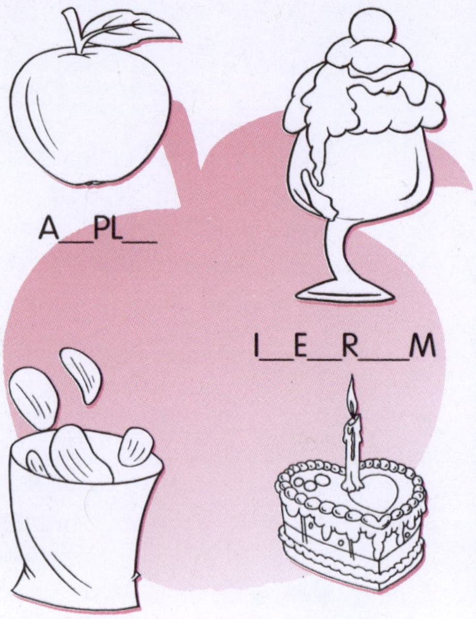

Connect the dots from 1 to 50 to find the animal and then colour the picture.

Decode each words from the pool below to complete the story.

Solve the sums and write your answers. Then, draw a path through all the '6s' to lead Bobby to his bones.

3 + 3 =	6 - 0 =	1 × 6 =	10 + 2 =
1 + 9 =	2 × 4 =	4 + 2 =	3 + 5 =
4 × 2 =	2 + 3 =	7 - 1 =	3 + 6 =
9 - 1 =	3 + 8 =	2 × 4 =	9 - 3 =

Write the missing numbers on the grid.

4	+		=	7
-		-		-
	+	1	=	
=		=		=
3	+		=	5

Write the correct tens and ones digit for each number.

12 = ☐ tens + ☐ ones

24 = ☐ tens + ☐ ones

11 = ☐ tens + ☐ ones

Help the duck reach the pond.

Connect the dots from 1 to 25 and colour the drawing.

Solve the multiplication problems and write your answers in the boxes provided.

Draw a path through the desert to lead camel to the oasis.

Fill the grid so that the numbers 1, 2, 3 and 4 appear in each vertical line in each horizontal line. No number can appear twice in a row. Follow the example that has been done for you.

Solve the sums on each key. The key that equals 5 is the one that opens the lock.

Connect the dots from 1 to 25 to see who jumps out of the water and then colour the picture.

Match the following.

Colour the picture brightly.

Count and write.

Fill in the blank circle to solve the multiplication problem.

5	×	◯	=	30
×		×		×
◯	×	◯	=	◯
=		=		=
15	×	◯	=	90

Unscramble the letters. Write the answers below.

afhtre ________

rbtoehr ________

rtmehr ________

istsre ________

Colour the same number of objects as shown in the box.

Name the dog's body parts.

How many insects can you count? Write the numbers in the box.

Bees ☐ Ladybugs ☐

Colour the highlighted alphabets that match the ones in the bubble.

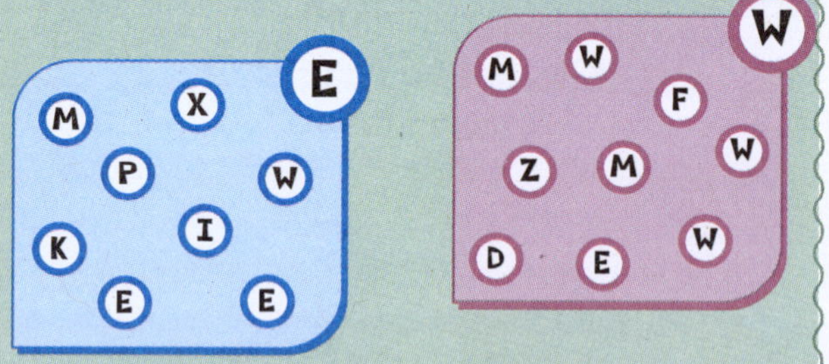

In each tray, circle the plate that contains the least amount of food.

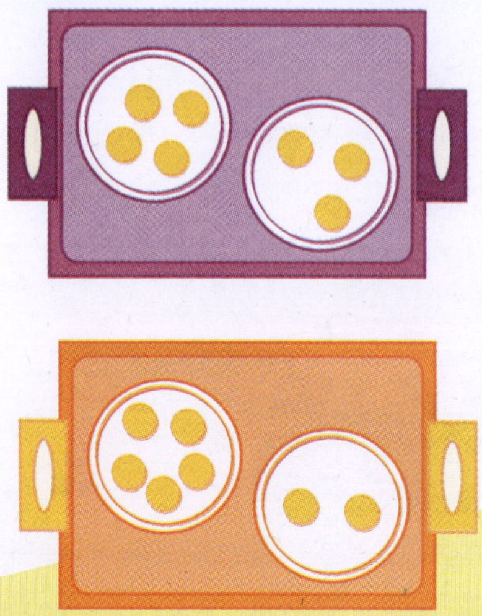

8 + 2 = ____ 10 + 3 = ____ 3 + 5 = ____

10 + 3 = ____ 6 + 2 = ____ 10 + 10 = ____

3 + 15 = ____ 3 + 5 = ____ 12 + 2 = ____

Solve the sums.

Help Mary and John count their respective objects.

_________ balles + _________ balles _________ balles in all

_________ crayons + _________ crayons _________ crayons in all

Match the identical shapes and colour them with same colour.

Trace the arrows and colour them.

Complete the patterns on both rectangles.

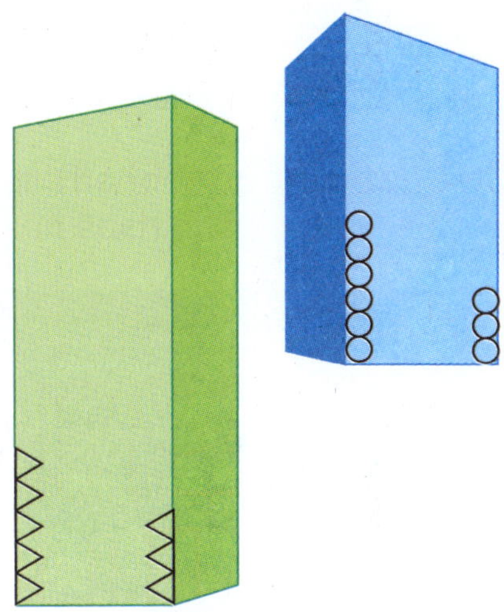

Colour the two identical boats.

Circle the objects that are made of wood.

Add the dots on the dice and write the answers.

Fill in the blanks to solve the sums.

2	+	4	=	____
6	+	____	=	8
4	+	____	=	10
8	+	4	=	____

Match the identical shapes and colour them with same colour.

Number the pictures in correct sequence.

Which piggy bank has the most money? Tick mark the correct option.

Write the names of these animals and colour them.

Colour the boat with colours of your choice.

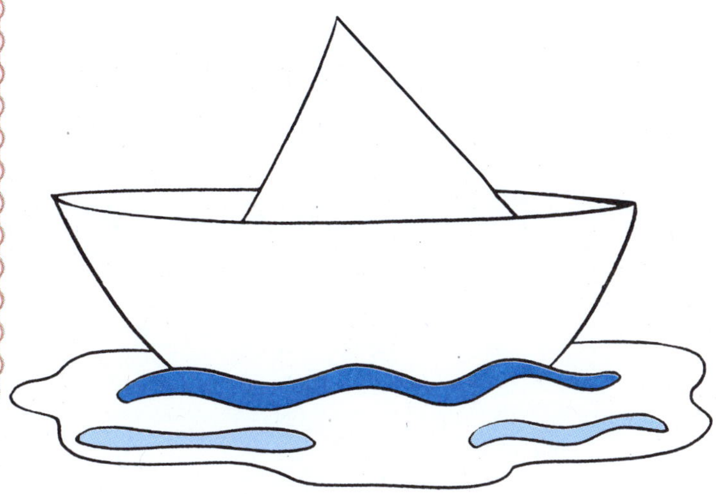

Help Leo to find his way out of the maze.

Trace the number 4.

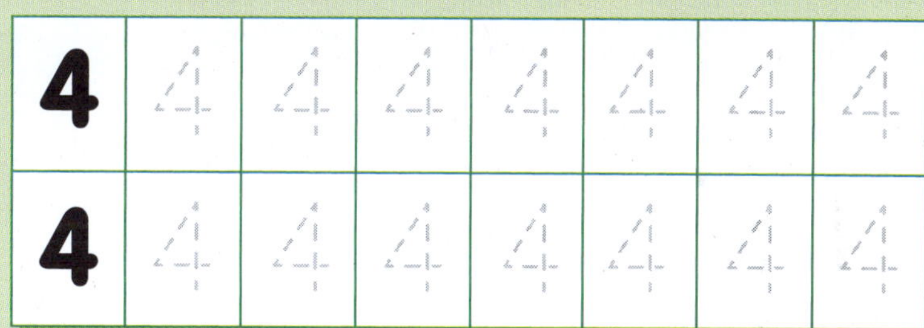

Fill in the vowels to make a word.

L_ _N B_T

CL_CK C_K_

B_CK_T N_B

R_S_ B_RD

a e i o u

Connect the dots and draw the largest possible square.

Trace and colour the animal.

Solve the sums and match them to their answers.

3 + 1	6	1 + 0
2	1 + 2	1
4 + 1	3	1 + 1
4	4 + 2	5

Complete the pattern in each row.

Match each cup with its saucer.

Count the objects in the picture and write them in the squares.

Colour the pictures and circle their names.

Bed
Rule

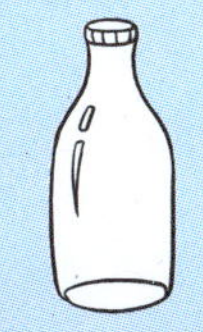

Cup
Bottle

Bath
Bus

Colour identical shapes with same colour.

Circle the living things and cross out the non-living ones.

Match each vegetable to its correct name.

mushroom

spinach

carrot

Cauliflower

onion

Which of these animals live on a tree?

Link sentences to the corresponding image.

- There are four bananas in this plate.
- Mark is holding two apples in his hands.
- Chloe is eating grapes.
- There is a box of strawberries on the table.

Match each image to its name.

hen

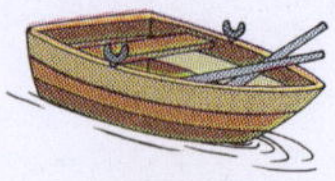

van

boat

trash can

Add the dots on the dice and write your answers.

Solve the riddles and match to the answers.

I have four legs. I'm sweet. I have petals.

If there are 9 blue glasses and 7 yellow-orange glasses, how many glasses are there in total?

Draw and colour the pictures as shown.

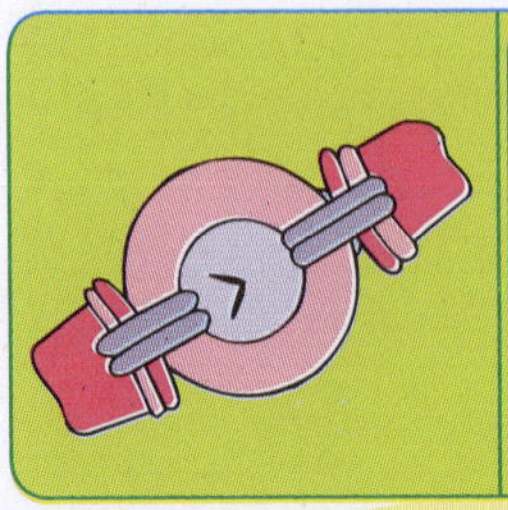

How many octopuses and fish do you see here?

 Octopus

 Fish

Circle the biggest fruit in each tray.

Circle the odd one out in each set.

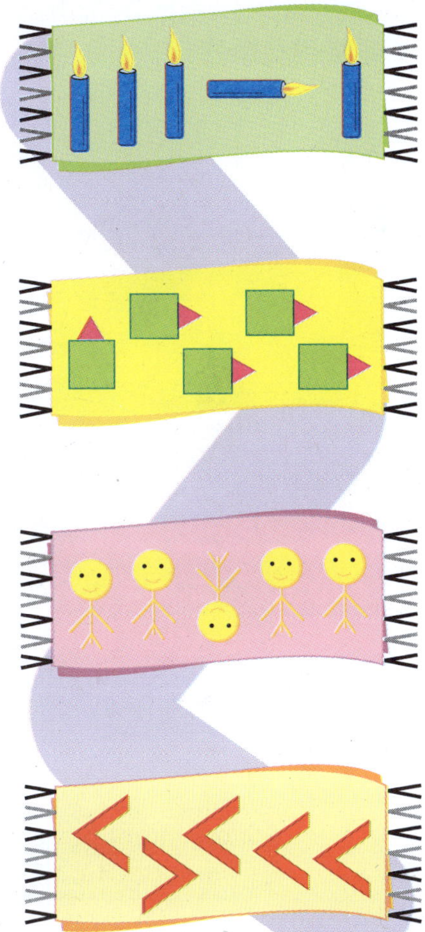

Follow the instructions to colour the giraffe.

1. Colour the face yellow.
2. Colour the spots black.

Circle the biggest object in each column.

Colour the dotted squares.

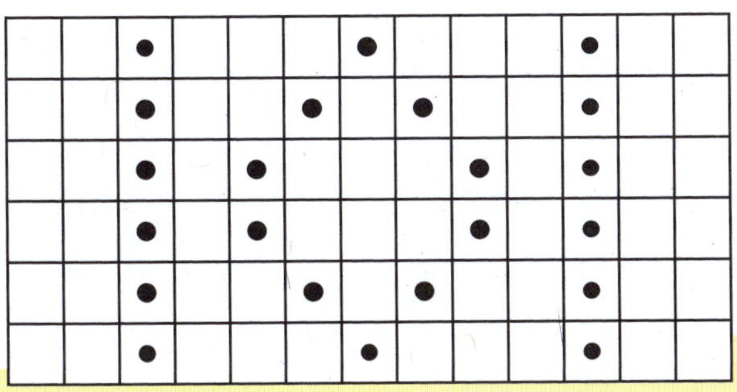

Unscramble the letters and write the words.

klbca _ _ _ _ _

der _ _ _

lelwoy _ _ _ _ _ _

rwbno _ _ _ _ _

nereg _ _ _ _ _

eulb _ _ _ _

ehwti _ _ _ _ _

knip _ _ _ _

Start at the traffic light. Colour the cars in this order: red, yellow, green and blue.

Mr Kaul needs help to deliver mail. Solve the sums and match each envelope to the right house.

Connect the dots.

How many pair of gloves can you spot? Colour them all.

Complete the series in each row.

1, 3, 5, _____, _____, _____, _____

6, 9, 12, _____, _____, _____, _____

17, 19, 21, _____, _____, _____, _____

6, 8, 10, _____, _____, _____, _____

Circle the reptile among these animals.

Decorate the geometric shaped box.

In each tray, circle the plate that contains the most food.

Trace the letters.

a a a a a a

b b b b b b

c c c c c c

Trace the letters and write each letter twice.

F F G G H H

I I J J

Count the gloves in each row and write the correct answer.

Match the number names to the numbers and the correct number of dots.

four	10
two	6
ten	0
six	4
eight	8
zero	2

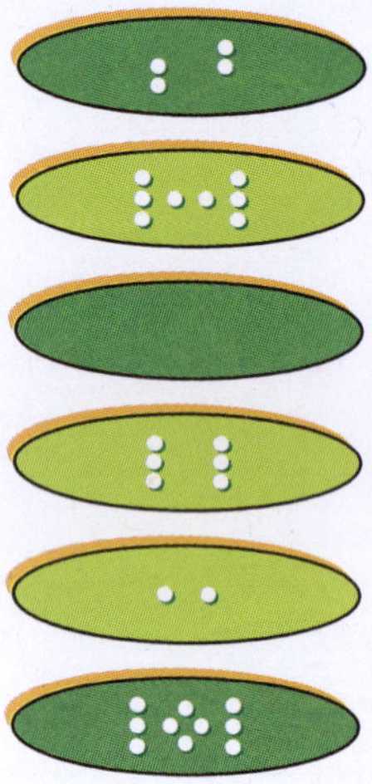

Draw and colour the deer as shown.

In each row, add the dots on two dice that add up to the number in the square. Circle them.

6

9

Solve the sums.

9 +8

8 +5

11 +4

13 +6

17 +3

10 +6

12 +5

14 +4

16 +6

Connect the fruits to their names and colour them.

Use the given letters and make the words having 2, 3, and 4 letters.

A L S E H

R N O T I

Words of 2 letters	Words of 3 letters	Words of 4 letters

Write the names of these animals and colour them.

....

....

....

....

....

Colour the picture. Also, draw some fish in the water and colour them.

Find and circle the names of the colours hidden in the grid.

BROWN
WHITE
RED
GREEN
ORANGE
BLUE
BLACK

B	R	O	W	N	K	K	K	K	K
L	M	D	R	J	W	H	I	T	E
R	E	D	A	C	R	K	L	E	G
O	F	H	S	O	G	R	E	E	N
O	R	A	N	G	E	G	T	K	Y
A	B	C	D	E	F	G	H	I	J
B	L	U	E	A	A	A	A	A	A
K	L	M	N	O	P	Q	R	S	T
U	V	W	X	Y	B	L	A	C	K
R	O	S	E	Z	H	R	W	K	N

Annie and Liam are playing with shapes. Help them colour all triangles ▲ blue, all circles ● red and all squares ■ green. Now, count the number of shapes each set has and add them up.

□ __ + __ = __ △ __ + __ = __ ○ __ + __ = __

□ __ + __ = __ △ __ + __ = __ ○ __ + __ = __

Write the names of these animals. Circle the one with a striped coat.

Write 5 words that rhyme with 'cat'.

Count each object below. Write the number.

Match each picture with its correct name. Also, colour them.

How many beads do you need to draw to add up to the number in the box.

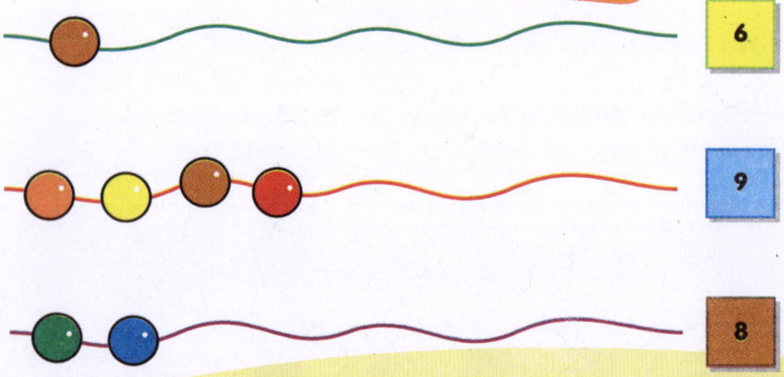

Trace the lines and colour the balls.

Match similar-sized pots and flowers.

Number the pictures in correct sequence.

Add the dots on the dice and write the answers.

Complete the picture.

Draw and colour the lady bug as shown.

Start at the traffic light. Colour the cars in this order: yellow, green, red and blue.

Help Ali add the numbers on the fish and circle the ones whose sum is 15.

Colour the picture and count the objects.

Find five errors in this drawing and circle them.

Count the number of objects in each set.

Circle the plate that contains less food.

Name these animals.

Change the vowel in each word. What new words do you get?

mast ______

Red ______

lake ______

Complete the patterns.

Match each capital letter with its lowercase.

In each row, add the dots on two dice that add up to the number in the square. Circle them.

Annie and Liam are playing with shapes. Help them colour all triangles ▲ blue, all circles ● red and all squares ■ green. Now, count the number of shapes each set has and add them up.

△ __ + __ = __ □ __ + __ = __ ○ __ + __ = __

□ __ + __ = __ △ __ + __ = __ ○ __ + __ = __

Match the sentences to the corresponding images.

Henry is eating an ice cream.

Lucy is playing with her dog.

Sam is reading a book.

Mila is sleeping.

Match each baby animal to its mother and then write the animals' name.

calf	______
puppy	______
kitten	______

Match the identical flowers.

Add and then match each magnet to its nail.

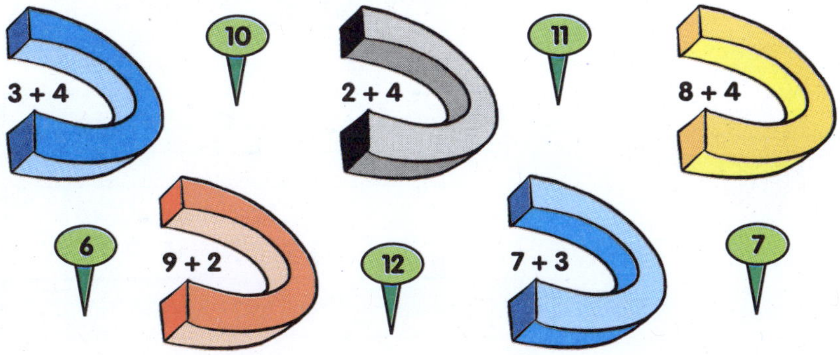

Circle the correct shadow of the bee.

Count and write the number of objects in each box.

Complete the patterns.

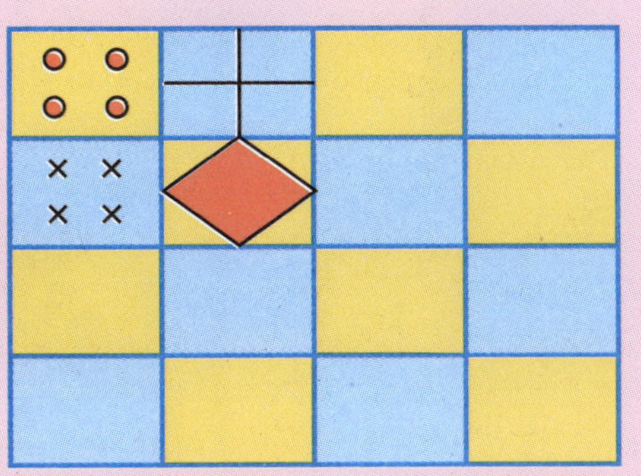

Write the names of these animals and circle the ones with a brown coat.

If there are 2 rows of cars with 7 cars parked in each row, how many cars are there in total?

Look at the list Riya made. Tick the right and cross the wrong calculations.

Tomates	11 kg + 5 kg = 15 kg	
Peas	9 kg + 3 kg = 13 kg	
Grapes	7 kg + 2 kg = 9 kg	
Carrots	4 kg + 7 kg = 12 g	
Potatoes	2 kg + 5 kg = 7 g	
Onions	8 kg + 2 kg = 10 g	
apples	6 kg + 8 kg = 14 g	
Melons	9 kg + 4 kg = 13 g	

Connect every sentence that describes the profession with its matching image.

I deliver mail, I am ...	an actor
I act in movies, I am ...	a pilot
I repair lamps and fans, I am ...	a mailman
People come to me when they are sick, I'm ...	a waiter
I serve diners at a restaurant. I am ...	an electrician
I fly airplanes, I am ...	a doctor

Solve the sums and help Fluffy find the matching socks.

Help Samar solve the Maths sum.

A bus is carrying eight girls and seven boys. The total number of children is:

_____ + _____ = _____

Colour the drawings according to the given code on the colour palette.

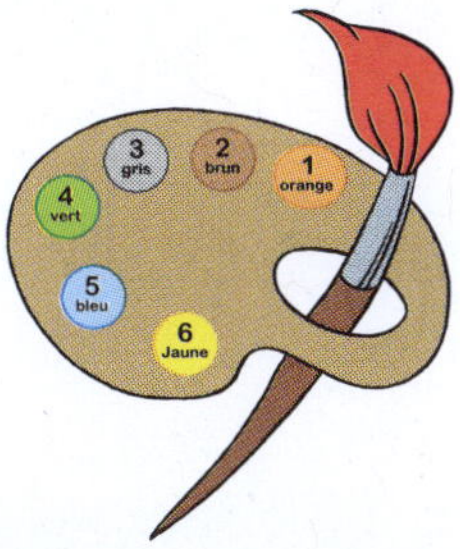

Circle the words that make you think of a party.

pencil
sleep
games
enjoy
hospital
read
gifts
photos
food
cake

Help Jacques solve the following addition sums.

What is 4+9 ?

What is the total of 3 and 6 ?

Find the sum of 2, 4 and 6 ?

What is the total of 8 and 7 ?

The red box contains 30 cards, and the blue box contains 20. In total, how many cards are there?

Observe the plates. Circle the largest fruit in each plate.

The postman needs help to deliver mail. Solve the sums and then match each envelope to the house.

Look at the numbers on the side of each car. Crack the colour code and colour them accordingly.

Help Samar solve the Maths sum.

There are three piles of bricks. The highest pile has 8 bricks, the smaller pile has 5 and the smallest pile has 3 bricks. How many bricks are there in total?

_____ + _____ = _____

Find two identical puppies.

Answer the questions given below.

How many pairs of toys are there?

There are ___ pairs of toys.

How many toys are there in total?

There ___ toys in all.

Count the number of objects in each row and match to the number names.

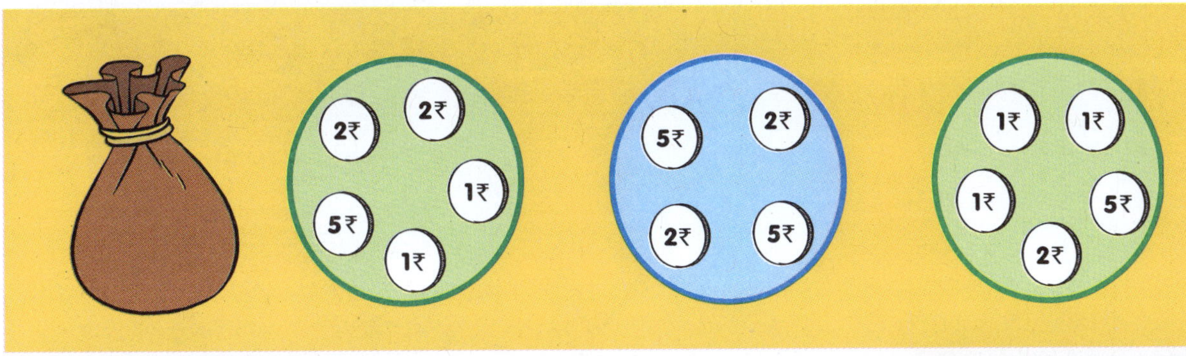

How many coins from each circle do you need to make ₹10? Colour them.

Draw and colour the giraffe as shown.

Match the numbers on each dartboard with their number names.

five three
seven four

four two
five three

Add 7 to each number and write the answer in the circle.

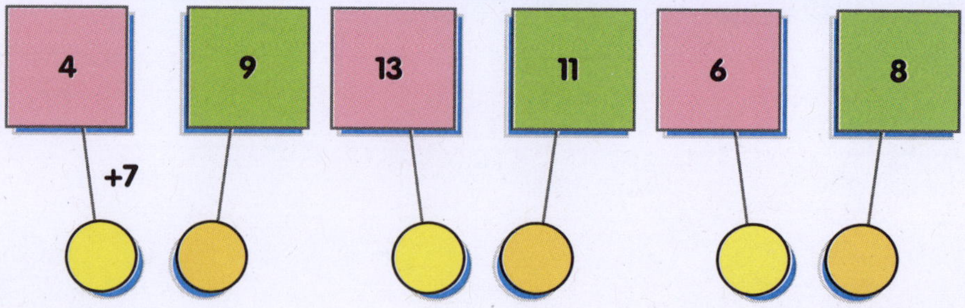

Read the months of the year and then write them in the correct order starting with January.

April | August | March
January | May | December
October | July | June
February | November | September

•I celebrate my birthday in __________.

•The month following my birthday month is ___________ .

•The month before my birthday is ___________.

Circle the animals that have spots.

Draw and colour the ball as shown.

Draw different

Colour the ball as indicated and complete the additions.

Colour 3 balls in blue colour.

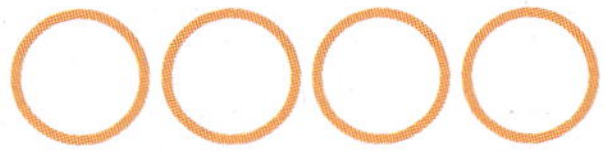

+ ___ = 4

Colour 3 balls in red.

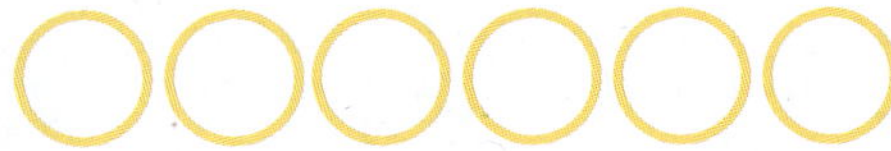

+ 3 = ___

Match the identical dinosaurs. Circle the odd pair.

Use the code to write the numbers for each object.

0	1	2	3	4	5	6	7	8	9
A	E	I	O	H	C	D	P	R	S

Trace the letters on the kites.

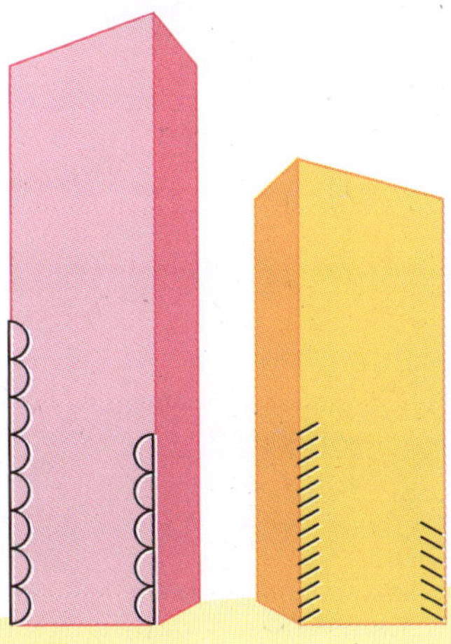

Observe and complete the patterns.

Colour the pictures.

There are 12 boys and 14 girls in the aircraft. How many children are there?

This building has 8 windows in the front and 7 windows in the rear. How many windows are there in all?

Help Samar solve the addition sums.

There are 12 books on the top shelf and four on the shelf below. How many books are there in total?

_____ + _____ = _____

Trace and colour the picture of ship with the colours of your choice.

Aayaan has four bags of 30 peanuts each. Each group gets 30 peanuts. Which group will get more peanuts for each child?

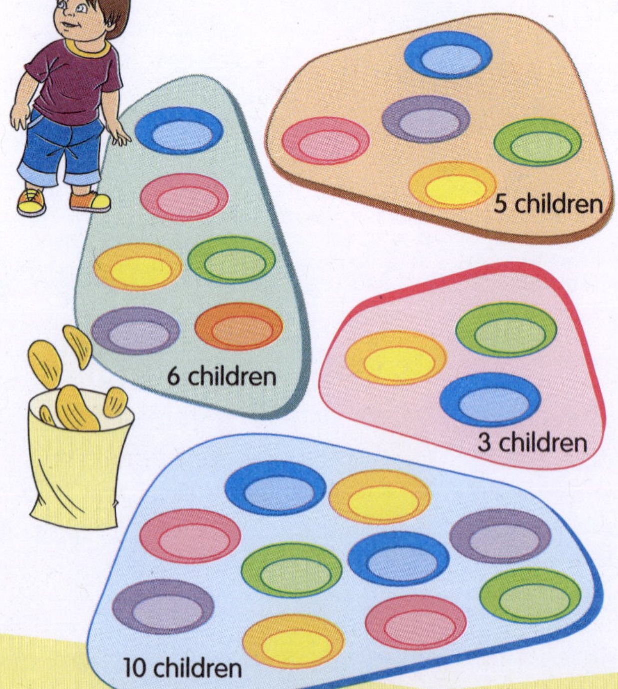

Trace the letters.

f f f f f f

g g g g g g

Number the houses on both sides of the road by adding 2 to the last number in the row.

Group the animals on the basis of their size, kind and where they live.

Snail, Seahorse,
Crab, Whale
Lion, Tiger,
Elephant, Rhino
Dog, Cat,
Rat, Cow
Parrot, Crow, Eagle
Hummingbird

Follow the instructions to put the parrots in cages.

If we put 5 parrots in 2 cages in a group of two. How many parrots will be left out?

If we put 7 parrots in 3 cages in a group of two. How many parrots will be left out?

Colour the indicated number of objects in each row.

4 

2 

Each child receives.

3 Candies   6 Candies   4 Candies   = ____ Candies in all.

5 Books   7 Books   2 Books   = ____ Books in all.

Help Samar solve the p.roblem

If a large fish tank has 5 big and 7 small fish, how many fish are there in total?

____ + ____ = ____

Tick the correct name of the image and colour it.

Photo
Pencil

Sun
Star

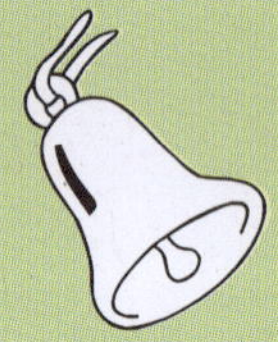

Hook
Bell

Circle the bigger object in each set

Write the missing numbers to solve the equations.

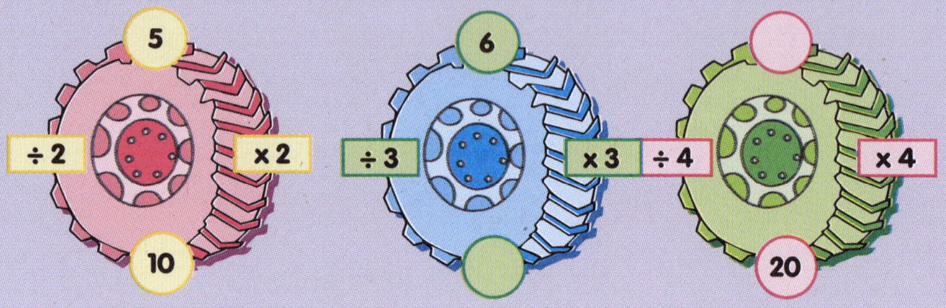

Can you match the pirates to their correct shadows?

Trace the patterns.

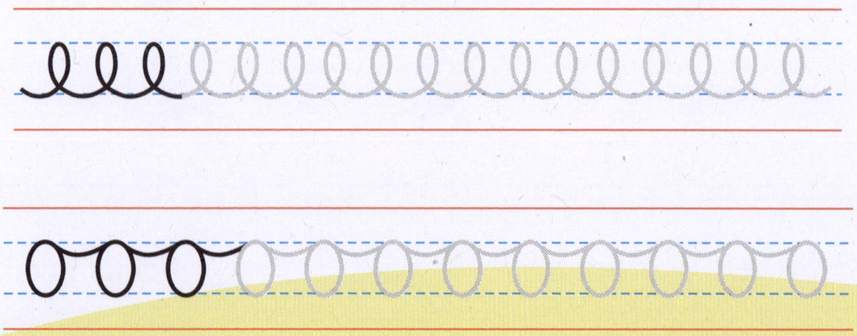

Perform operations and write the results on the screens.

Colour the trees.

Count and write how many trees are there.

Count and write the number of objects in each box.

How many animals of each kind are there on the farm?

Fill in the letters that come before and after the given letter.

before		after
______	g	______
______	c	______
______	m	______
______	k	______
______	x	______
______	r	______

Colour the same-looking plates in same colour.

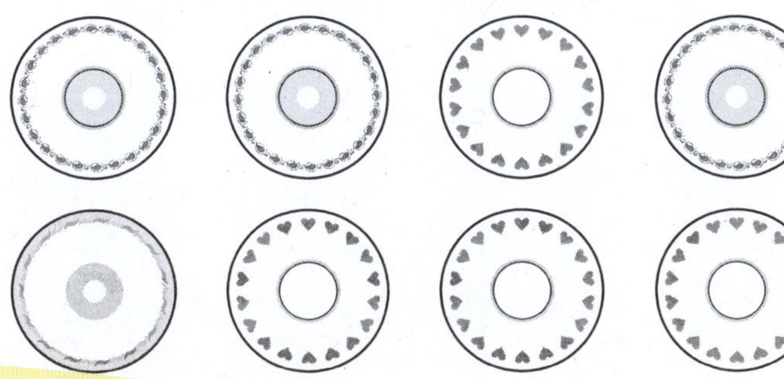

Find the correct Shadow

Colour the pictures as directed.

red, white, orange, purple, blue, green, yellow, black, pink, brown

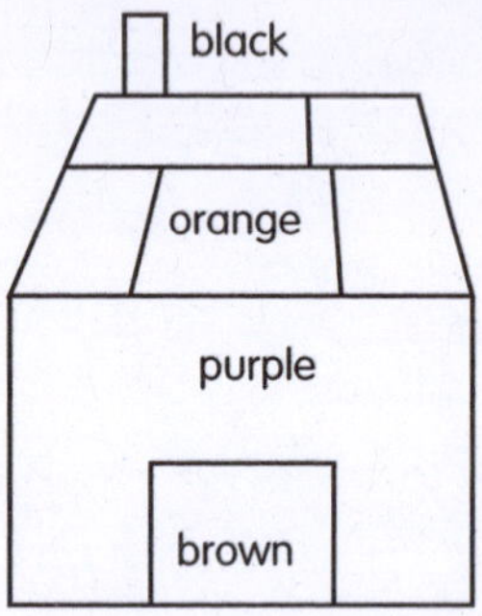

Trace the letters.

k k k k k k

r r r r r r

Form groups of 4 flowers and colour them. Complete the sentences.

9 flowers = ______ groups of 4 and remaining flowers = ______

11 flowers = ______ groups of 4 and remaining flowers = ______

Which piggy bank contains the least money? Add to check.

Complete the sequence with the numbers provided below.

Make as many words as possible with the word PHONES.

2 and 3 letter words

____
____
____

4-letter words

____
____
____

5-letter words

____
____
____

Trace the letters.

d d d d d d d

e e e e e e e

Colour the animals.

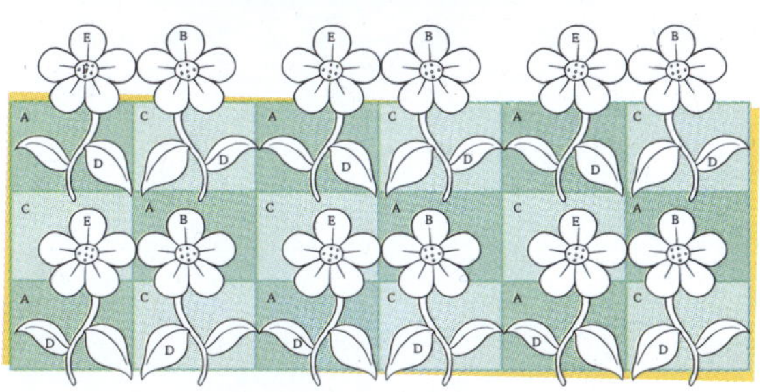

Colour the flowers as indicated.

Colour Code

A-brown B-pink C-black D-green E-red F-yellow

Match the alphabets in the column with their correct lowercase.

c g e d l q

_ _ _ _ _ _

m j c r i v

_ _ _ _ _ _

A	N
B	O
C	P
D	Q
E	R
F	S
G	T
H	U
I	V
J	W
K	X
L	Y
M	Z

t b e k u s

_ _ _ _ _ _

t h p q r y

_ _ _ _ _ _

Count and fill in the blanks to complete the equation.

Match the missing letters to complete the names of the months on the fish.

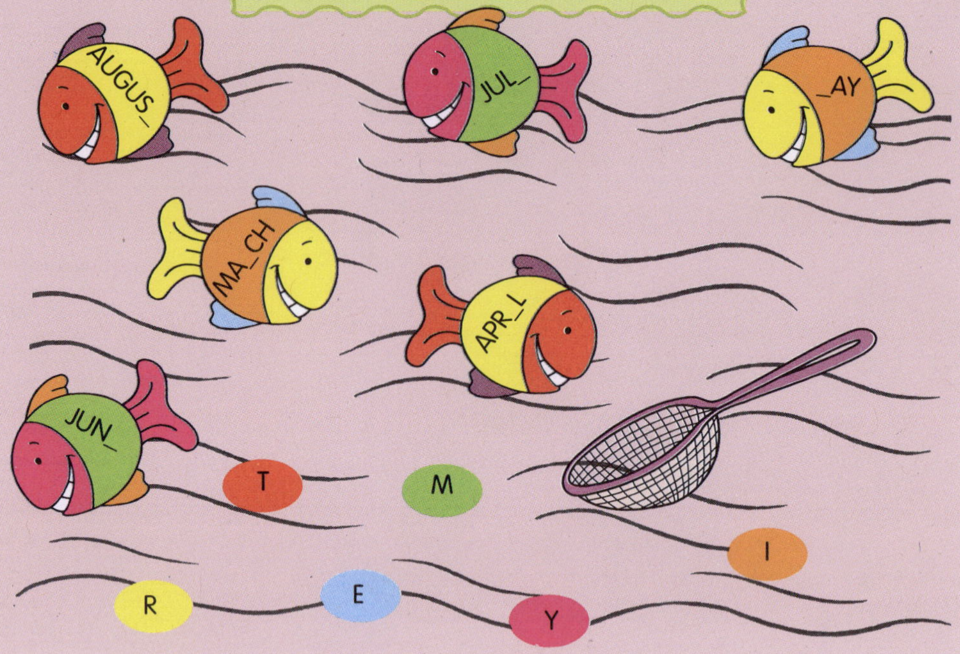

Look at the pictures, write the missing letters to complete their names.

G_f_

B_l_

D_o_

After eating food, John takes a nap.

When Camille comes back from school, she sits for sometime with her mom.

Camille and John go to the park, where they meet their friends. They play a lot.

Their father picks them from the park in the car.

Camille and John drink a glass of milk before going to the park.

Dad puts the children in bed and tells them a story.

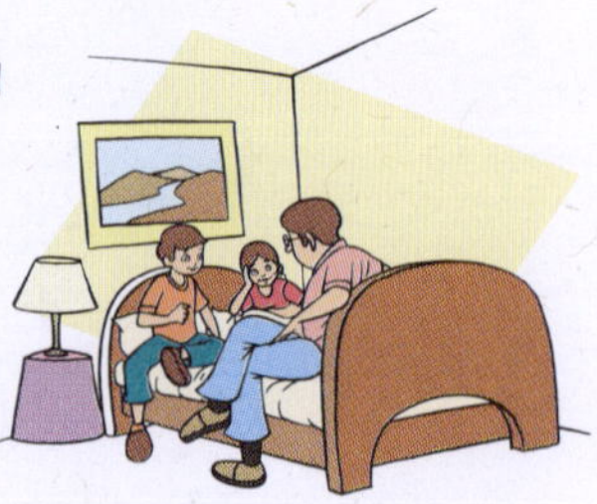

The whole family have supper together and watch TV.

In a word, answer the questions.

1. What does John do after dinner? ___________
2. Camille sits with whom she when she comes home from school?___________
3. What do Camille and John drink before going to the park. ___________
4. Who joins Camille and John in the park? ___________
5. Who picks Camille and John from the park? ___________
6. What does the family do while eating supper?___________

Match each animal to the first letter of its name.

Colour and then add the balloons to complete the sum.

Match each animal with its name and colour it.

Trace the words.

in in in in in

an an an an an an

Trace the dotted lines and write the number 11.

11	11	11	11	11
11				

How many parrots in one cage?

____ parrots are remaining.

Divide 14 parrots in 3 cages.

Follow the instructions in each box.

Divide 9 parrots in 2 cages.

How many parrots in one cage?

____ parrots are remaining.

Bill skips 25 times and Henry 10 times. How many times did they skip in total.

Colour by number.

- 1 - yellow
- 2 - purple
- 3 - green
- 4 - dark blue
- 5 - light blue
- 6 - orange
- 7 - red
- 8 - black

Each child receives:

4 pencils 8 pencils 3 pencils = _ _ pencils at all

6 roses 9 roses 3 roses = _ _ roses at all

Find five differences in the two pictures.

Count the objects in the picture and fill in the blanks.

Write the missing letters.

_iraffe

_umper

Shopping list

rice
25 Kg ÷ 5 = ______ Kg.

flour
18 Kg ÷ 9 = ______ Kg.

sugar
24 Kg ÷ 6 = ______ Kg.

onions
30 Kg ÷ 5 = ______ Kg.

Potatoes
20 Kg ÷ 10 = ______ Kg.

Complete divisions.

Trace the given letters.

m m m m m m m

n n n n n n n

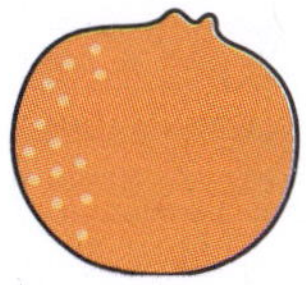

o o o o o o o

Trace the letters and write them twice.

A A B B C C

D D E E

Nadia told Mira where she lives. Follow her instructions and trace the path around the town with Mira.

- Place yourself on the word START.
- Go straight and take the first street on the right.
- At the intersection, turn left. you will see
- Shopping Centre on your right.
- Continue straight on. You will have the forest on your right.
- Not far into the forest, you will see a street on the left. Do not take it. Take the Second street on the left.
- Nadia lives in the first house on right.

Circle the animals with the same colour. Also match the animals whose names begin with the same letters.

Colour the flowers and form groups of four. Count groups and the flowers that remain.

15 flowers = ______ groups of 4 and______ remaining flowers

17 flowers = ______ groups of 4 and______ remaining flowers

Trace the dotted lines and write the number 8.

8	8	8	8	8
8				

Count the objects on each plate, on both tables, and complete the equation.

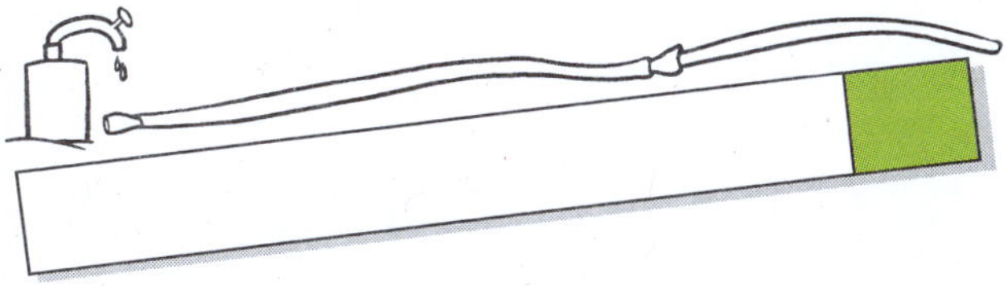

Jay uses two pipes to water the lawn. If the length of the first pipe is 7 metres and the second one's 4 metres, what is the total length?

Help Bulbul count each object.

Trace the letters and practice.

r r r r r r

s s s s s s

t t t t t t

Colour, count and then add the balloons to complete the sum.

Write the missing letters to complete the words.

Dr__m

H__art

Cag__

Complete the animals by drawing their missing parts.

Write the missing digit on each tyre

Trace the words.

or or or or or or

at at at at at at

Use the code to write the numbers for each object.

0	1	2	3	4	5	6	7	8	9
A	E	I	O	H	C	D	P	R	S

Make your own words and write the code.

_ _ _ _   _ _ _   _ _ _ _ _

Observe the animals in the zoo.

Find their names in the grid.

A	K	K	D	O	O	G	L	L
M	O	N	K	E	Y	Z	Z	S
A	G	G	D	D	F	F	H	N
J	K	T	I	G	E	R	A	A
A	B	C	D	E	F	A	H	K
J	B	I	R	D	O	T	E	E
S	S	G	F	F	T	T	I	I
E	L	E	P	H	A	N	T	R
A	B	C	D	E	F	G	H	I
J	S	Q	U	I	R	R	E	L

Help Nyra solve the following.

7 + 6 + 9 = ?

Find the sum of 4, 6 and 7.

6 + 9 + 12 = ?

What is the sum of 5, 9 and 11?

Circle the smallest number in each of the boxes.

2 7 4

8 5 3

6 9 4

Circle the names of the objects and colour them.

tent
boat

ice-cream
popcorn

lamp
bulb

Timtim and Sarah are playing with numbers. Can you help Timtim colour even numbers purple and Sarah colour the odd numbers yellow?

Solve the sums.

Practice cursive writing.

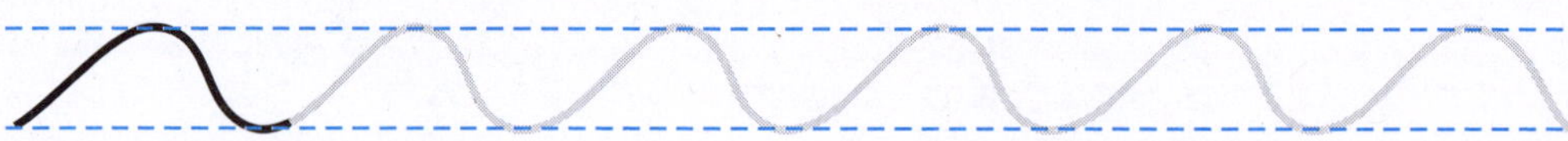

Colour the elephants.

Count and fill in the blanks to complete the addition sum.

Help the frog reach the ant.

Help Nyra add up numbers.

Complete the sums.

1	+	____	=	2
3	+	____	=	8
5	+	2	=	____
7	+	1	=	____

Help the ghost reach the mummy by stepping on boxes where the difference is 5. Trace the path.

	7-2=	4-3=	7-3=	3-1=
	8-6=	9-4=	9-3=	7-1=
5-3=	0+1=	5-1=	7-2=	
9-8=	6-3=	5-1=	9-6=	

Trace the letters.

p p p p p p

q q q q q q

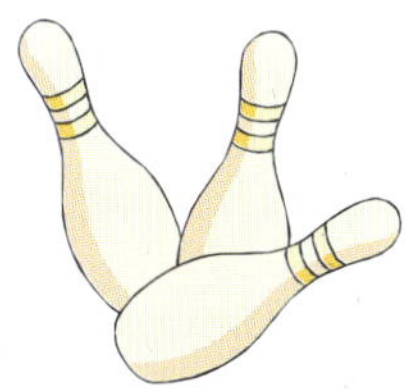

Match each animal to its shadow.

Choose the correct number and complete the following additions.

2 + ____ = 6   5   4   ____ + 3 = 8

3 + ____ = 9   6   3   ____ + 4 = 7

Solve the given equations and write how many will be remaining.

17 pens 17 ÷ 5 = _____ Y _____ Remaining pens ______ pens.

9 pens 9 ÷ 5 = _____ Y _____ Remaining pens ______ pens.

13 pens 13 ÷ 5 = _____ Y _____ Remaining pens ______ pens.

21 pens _____ ÷ _____ = _____ Y _____ Remaining pens ______ pens.

27 pens _____ ÷ _____ = _____ Y _____ Remaining pens ______ pens.

18 pens _____ ÷ _____ = _____ Y _____ Remaining pens ______ pens.

Help Advay sort the singular and plural words. Tick the singular words and circle the plural words.

Dishes, Stores, Box, Dog, Babies, Bottle, Flat, Dogs, Noise, Boxes, Bottles, Toys, Toy, Noise, Baby, Store, Chair, Girls, Chairs, Daughter

Fill in the blanks to create words.

B_r_s

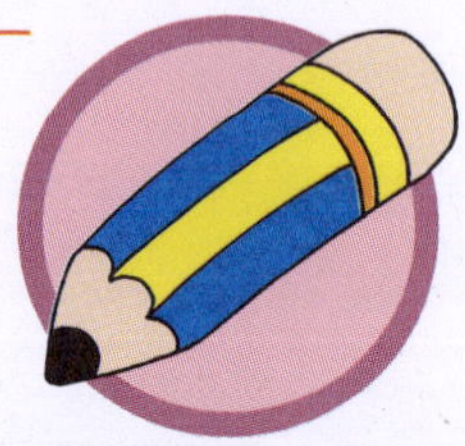

P_nc_l

Read the sentences given below and answer the questions.

Pia and Jeh wake up. They brush their teeth and groom themselves and have their breakfast.

Pia takes her school bag and leaves the house to wait for the school bus.

Ryan plays at home.

Back at home, Jeh eats his dinner.

At school, Pia answers questions her teacher asks. She loves mathematics.

Mom goes shopping with Jeh.

Write 'True' or 'False'.

1. Pia goes to school after eating breakfast.________
2. Pia goes to school by bus. ________
3. Jeh plays with his animals home. ________
4. Pia hates mathematics. ________
5. Jeh goes shopping with Mom. ________
6. Mom leaves Jeh at the supermarket. ________

Trace the letters.

h h h h h h

i i i i i i

j j j j j j

Fill in the missing letters.

G_a_es

A_e

Colour the castle according to the given reference.

Colour the picture and complete the sentence.

Sayarah reads for two hours in the morning and one hour in the evening.
How many hours does she read in all?

In the two groups circle two numbers that would make up 7 and 9.

Write the missing number on each tyre.

Trace the letters and write them twice.

K K L L M M

N N O O

P P Q Q R R

S S T T

Count and write total number of animals in each set.

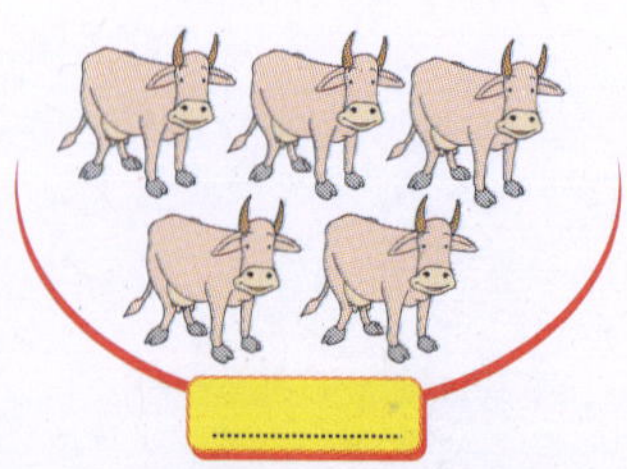

Trace the words.

so so so so so so

do do do do do do

to to to to to to

Each car can carry three children. Solve these problems.

If there are 7 children:
They need __ cars.
__ child/children will be left behind.

If there are 11 children:
They need __ cars.
__ child/children will be left behind.

If there are 15 children:
They need __ cars.
__ child/children will be left behind.

The teacher explains the rules of the class to the for children. Read them and answer questions.

Answer "yes" or "no."

- Can you run in the classroom? _______
- Can you be mean to your classmates? _______
- Should you watch your belongings?_______
- Should the class must be in order? _______
- In the morning, when you reach your class, should you paint in silence? _______
- In two sentences, explain what you like most about your school.

____

____

Fill in the missing letter to complete the word.

_ron

_kirt

Read Tenzing's directions and draw his room.

1. The bed is in the right corner at the bottom.
2. My office and my work chair are to the left of the bed.
3. The bed has drawers.
4. Next to the cage of birds, there is a shelf.
5. There is a rug in the centre of the room, with lots of toys on it.
6. The cabinet is in the left corner at the bottom.

Draw the house and colour it too.

Trace the pattern and practice.

Form groups on the basis of colour.

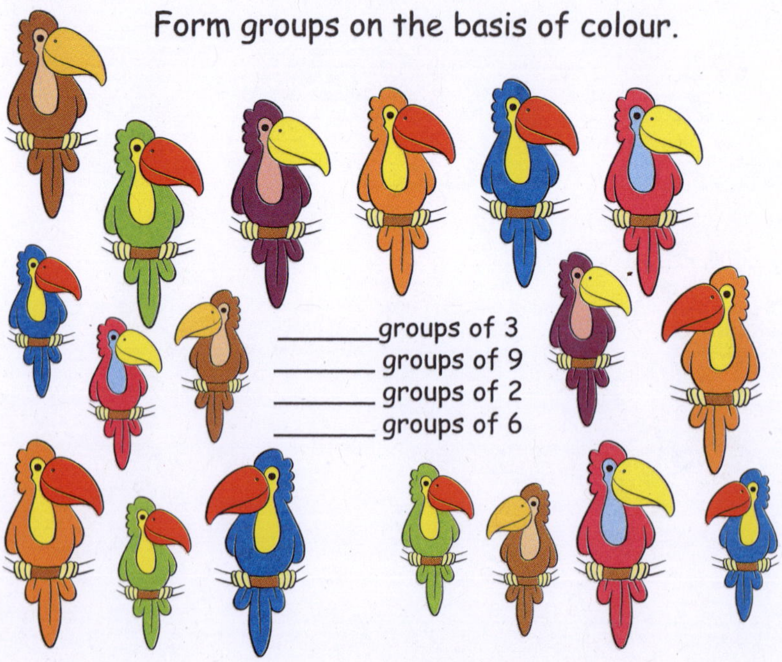

_______ groups of 3

_______ groups of 9

_______ groups of 2

_______ groups of 6

_______ Total Birds

Match each t-shirt and its design.

Complete these divisions:

3 ÷ 3 = ____________

6 ÷ 3 = ____________

9 ÷ 3 = ____________

12 ÷ 3 = ____________

15 ÷ 3 = ____________

18 ÷ 3 = ____________

Help the pirate reach the treasure chest by tracing the correct path.

Solve the sums and match each answer to the correct number on the boats.

28 ÷ 7

36 ÷ 4

28 ÷ 4

40 ÷ 10

45 ÷ 5

14 ÷ 2

Trace the letters.

y y y y y y

z z z z z z

15 pens

15 ÷ 5

____

25 pens

25 ÷ 5

____

Draw as many beads as indicated in the squares.

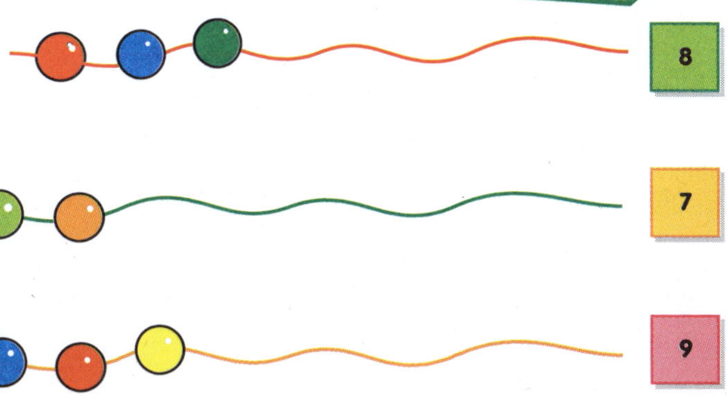

Let us study the different ways to divide the flowers.

Total number of flowers._______

Divide the flowers equally in two vases.

12 ÷ 2 = _____

Divide the flowers equally in three vases.

12 ÷ 3 = _____

Solve the sums on the cars and colour them using the colour code.

Colour the puppets and circle the first letter of their names in the string of the letters below.

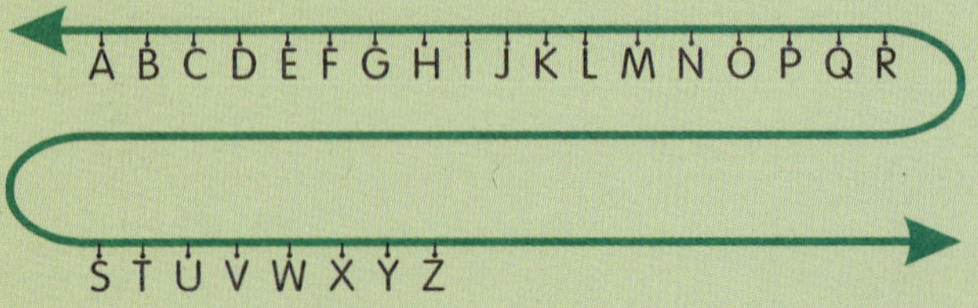

Help Kiara get out of the jungle. Add 1 in each box to find the way out.

Each car can carry three children. Solve the problems given below.

5 children in all.
_____ car
_____ the rest of the children.

18 children in all.
_____ car
_____ the rest of the children.

Solve these problems.

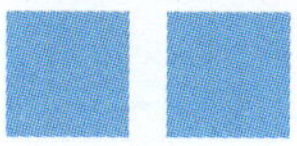 +  = _____

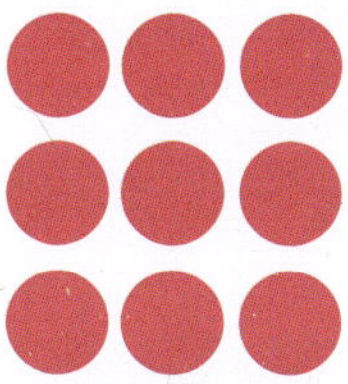 – 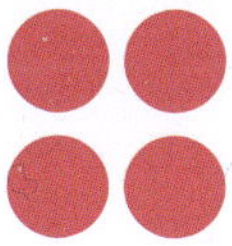 = _____

Colour in the wall as indicated.

There are 16 red bricks and 5 blue bricks. The total number brick is.

Trace the dotted lines and then write the number.

9	9	9	9	9
9				

Trace the dotted lines and then write the number 10.

10	10	10	10	10
10				

Trace the letters.

W W W W W W

X X X X X X

Circle the odd one out in each row.

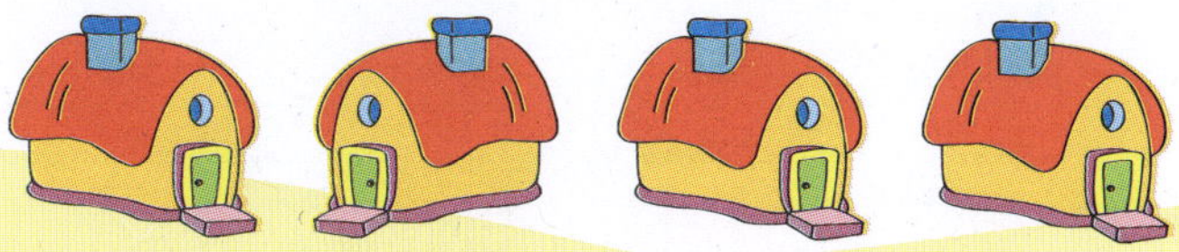

Form groups.

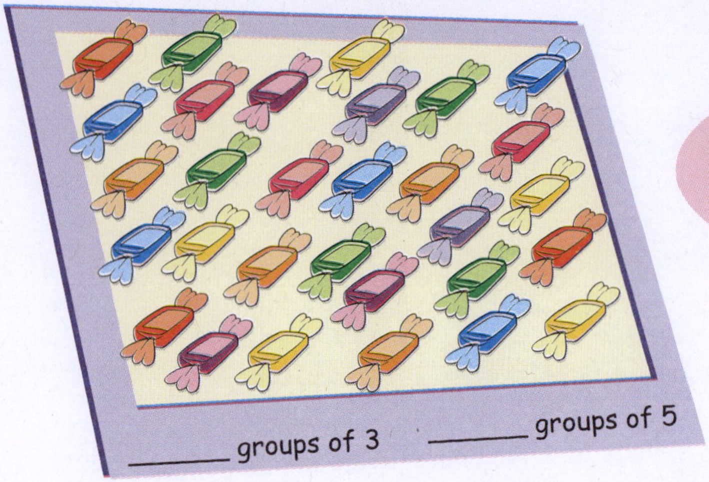

_______ groups of 3 _______ groups of 5

Solve the sums and match them to the correct answers.

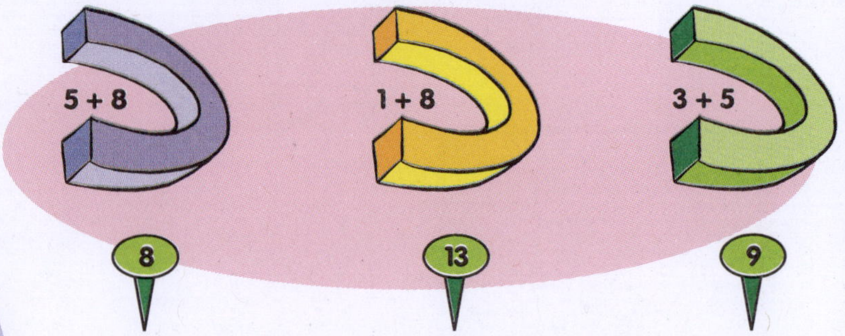

Colour and connect each pair of socks to the children to whom they belong.

Find Kian's score.

10 + 7 + 5 + 2 = ___   8 + 6 + 4 + 2 = ___

Colour the animals in the food chain.

Juhi walks 28 steps forward and then takes 8 more steps. Find the total number of forward steps she takes.

Number the months in their right order. Circle the months with R in their names.

Read the instructions, complete the drawing and colour it.

1. Draw a door and add two windows to the house.
2. Draw four fish in the pond.
3. Draw an apple under the tree.
4. Draw a boy playing with a ball.

Complete each sequence by adding 2 to each number.

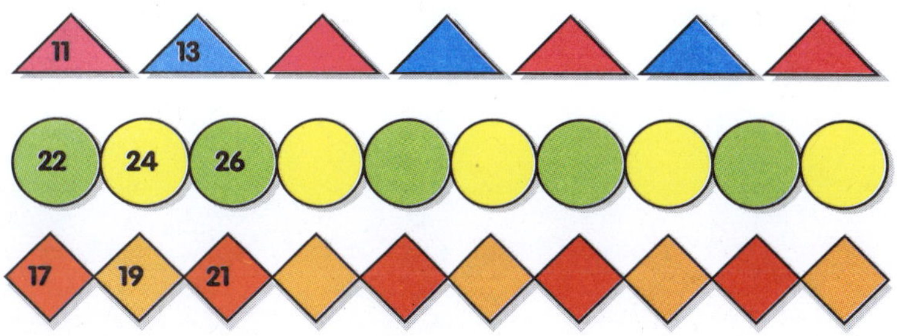

Solve and match the sums to the answers.

48 ÷ 8

16 ÷ 2

20 ÷ 4

32 ÷ 4

54 ÷ 9

30 ÷ 6

Trace the letters.

U U U U U U

V V V V V V

Timpy shut down his restaurant and shared all the objects he owned equally with his friends. Solve the sums to find how many objects each friend got.

Water glasses
60 ÷ 5 = _____

Mugs
35 ÷ 5 = _____

Ranges
60 ÷ 5 = _____

Tables
16 ÷ 4 = _____

Juice bottles
28 ÷ 4 = _____

Spoons
80 ÷ 4 = _____

Knives
55 ÷ 5 = _____

Chairs
75 ÷ 3 = _____

Plates
80 ÷ 4 = _____

Match each word to its opposite.

small	long
thin	night
day	bad
short	thick
black	big
good	white

Perform the additions and colour boxes using the colour code given.

18 + 7	11 + 8	14 + 5	30 + 8	5 + 2
17 + 2	3 + 4	31 + 6	15 + 8	10 + 6
15 + 15	28 + 6	8 + 1	6 + 4	14 + 3
16 + 3	13 + 9	11 + 6	12 + 7	13 + 5

Karl's score.

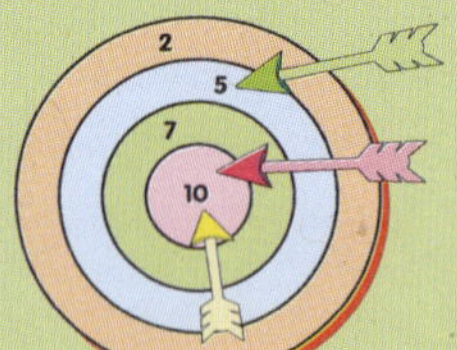

10 + 7 + 5 + 2 = ___

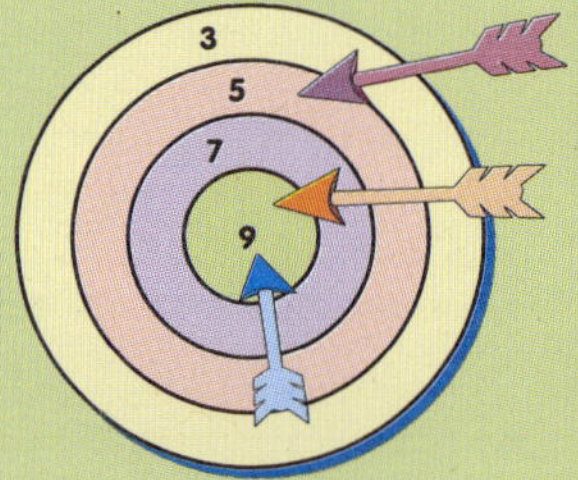

9 + 7 + 5 + 3 = ____

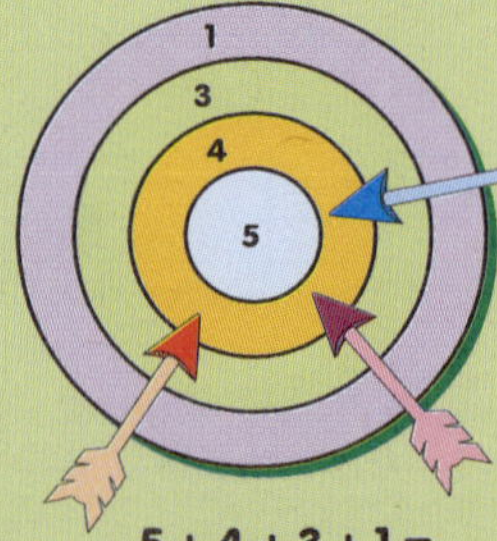

5 + 4 + 3 + 1 = ____

In each row, cross the odd one out.

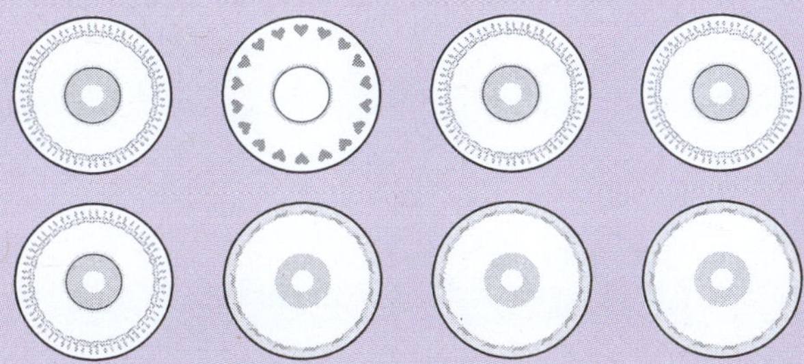

Find the names of colours in the grid and circle them.

R	O	U	G	E	G	L	M	Z	Q
O	B	C	R	P	J	W	E	E	A
S	I	O	I	B	L	E	U	I	O
E	O	P	S	J	A	U	N	E	Z
D	K	J	L	S	U	V	O	P	M
T	I	B	R	U	N	I	I	T	Z
J	K	O	Y	P	Y	P	R	U	W
B	L	A	N	C	H	O	I	S	P

RED, BLACK, WHITE, BLUE

Jade has two vases. Help her divide the flowers between the two vases.

Observe the picture and read the sentences. Circle the correct one.

There is a bird on the branch.

There are several birds on the branch.

Fishes are above the water.

Fish is under the water.

Circle the odd one out.

Let's do division!

30 divided by 2 = ____

20 divided by 5 = ____

16 divided by 8 = ____

21 divided by 3 = ____

16 divided by 4 = ____

12 divided by 6 = ____

Salman reads only half of each book. How many pages did she read?

32 pages
Salman read ___ pages.

28 pages
Salman read ___ pages.

48 pages
Salman read ___ pages.

Match each quilt to the cloth it uses.

Count the objects in each set and write the total number. Now write how much is half of it.

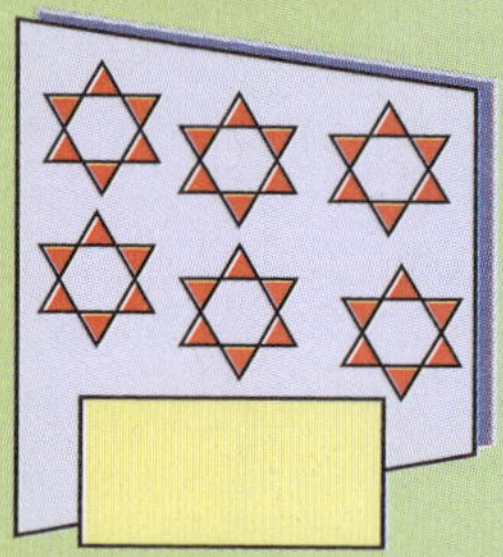

half = _____

half = _____

half = _____

Match each baby animal to its mother and then write its name.

Perform the additions and colour boxes using the colour code given.

14 + 8	2 + 8	10 + 10	27 + 4	6 + 2
21 + 6	20 + 3	5 + 4	7 + 3	26 + 3
12 + 4	17 + 6	9 + 2	18 + 2	28 + 4

Circle the letters that are identical to the reference in the corner.

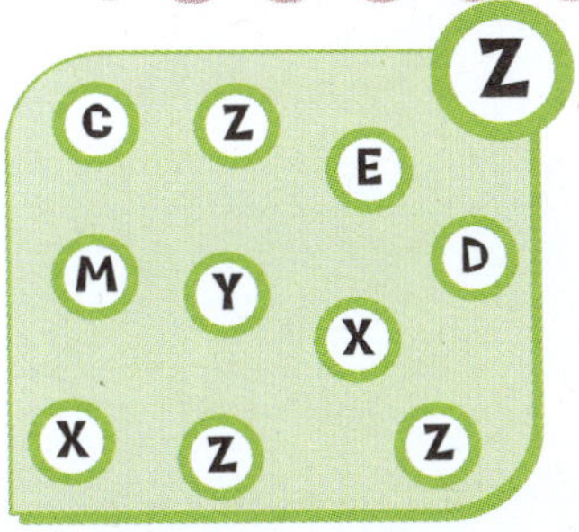

Lucy needs you! Help her write on each paper the two letters of the alphabet after the given letter.

Draw the balloons in the hand of Arthur to bring the total given.

Complete the book with personal information.

My notebook

My name is

I am ___ years

I live with ________

____

My favourite subject is

____

I like playing ______

with ____________

____

Circle the words that describe you.

Happy	Small	Confident
Long hair	Tall	Short hair
Calm	Sad	

Match the pictures that relate to each other.

Circle the smallest number in each box.

Solve the division sums.

15 ÷ 3 = _____ 6 ÷ 3 = _____ 24 ÷ _____ = 12

21 ÷ 3 = _____ 30 ÷ 3 = _____ 10 ÷ _____ = 5

9 ÷ 3 = _____ 18 ÷ 2 = _____ _____ ÷ 3 = 6

Rehaan and Maanya want to share their chocolates equally. Write how many chocolates each will get.

Connect the dots and find out which animal is this.

Fill in the missing letter.

There was a power outage at the grocery store. View how many fruits were damaged.

Use the numbers on the scale to answer the questions.

0 1 2 3 4 5 6 7 8 9 10

forward ⟶

backward ⟵

If you are on number 4 and you move 4 more, you will come to ______

You're at number 2 and jump 3 digits forward to ______

You are on number 6 and you fall by 3 numbers, you are now on ______

If you add 2 to the number 2, you will get to ______

If you add 4 to number 1, you get ______

You're at 6, add 1 = ______ .

You're at 3, add 4 = ______ .

You're at 8, subtract 2 = ______ .

You're at 7, add move 3 more= ______ .

Write the equations, solve and write the answers.

___ ÷ ___ = ___

___ ÷ ___ = ___

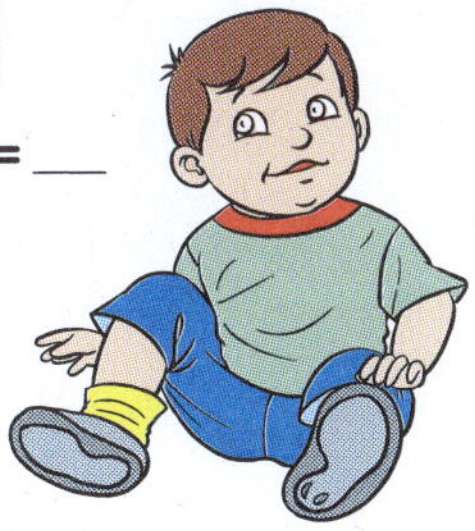

Solve the sums and colour the cars by following the colour code.

Write a new word for each letter of FRUIT. Each word should begin with that letter.

1. F

2. R

3. U

4. I

5. T

8 : 15 → ______

4 : 10 → ______

10 : 08 → ______

9 : 12 → ______

Add 10 minutes to find the new time.

Write the names of these animals.

Connect each kite to the child to whom it belongs.

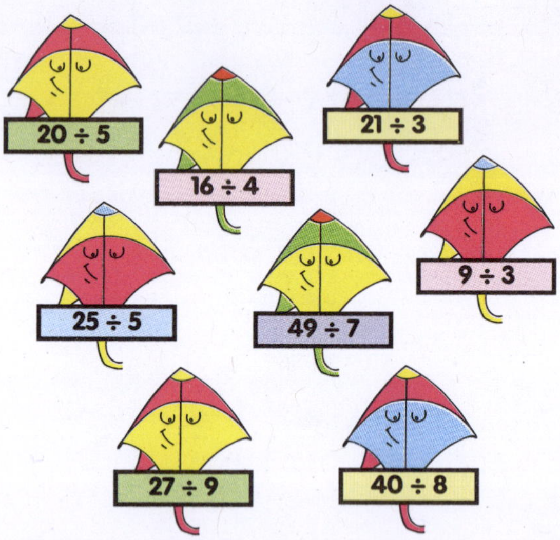

Choose the antonym (opposite) in the basket and write it.

top______

open______

seated______

small______

asleep______

left______

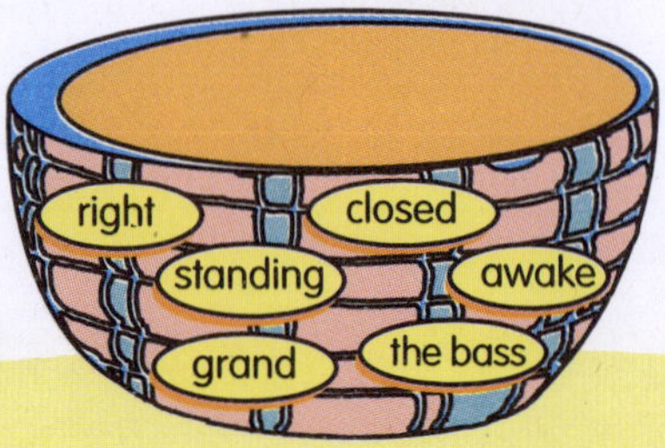

Jaspreet has read only half of each book. How many pages has she read?

34 pages
Jaspreet read ______ pages.

16 pages
Jaspreet read ______ pages.

26 pages
Jaspreet read ______ pages.

Solve the sums and colour the kites according to the given colour codes.

Rehaan and Maanya want to share their chocolates equally. Write how many chocolates each will get.

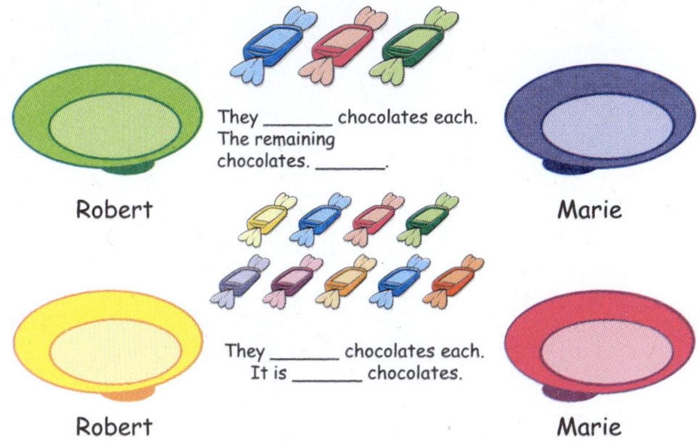

Form different groups:

______ groups of 2

______ groups of 3

______ groups of 4

______ groups of 8

______ groups of 3

______ groups of 5

______ groups of 10

Observe the picture and read the sentences.
Circle the correct sentence.

Complete the drawing.

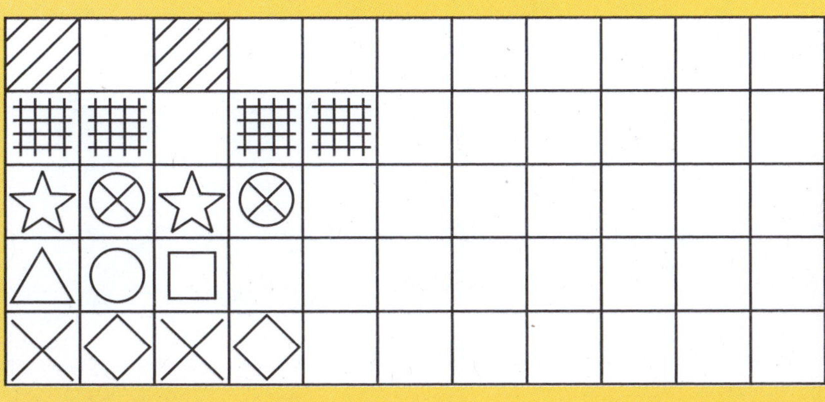

Match the children to the bus that has the same letter as the one they are holding.

Half of the mushrooms, onions and tomatoes are damaged. A quarter of the ladyfinger, carrots and peas have rotted. Write the names of the vegetables that cannot be eaten.

Rotten vegetables

Mushrooms: 12 ÷ 2 = _____ kg

Onions: _____ ÷ _____ = _____ kg

Tomates: _____ ÷ _____ = _____ kg

Ladyfinger: _____ ÷ 4 = _____ kg

Carottes: _____ ÷ _____ = _____ kg

Peas: _____ ÷ _____ = _____ kg

Use the letters on the monkeys' placards to make as many words as you can.

There are 8 parrots and 9 crows in the sky. How many birds are there in total?

Circle the odd one out in each series.

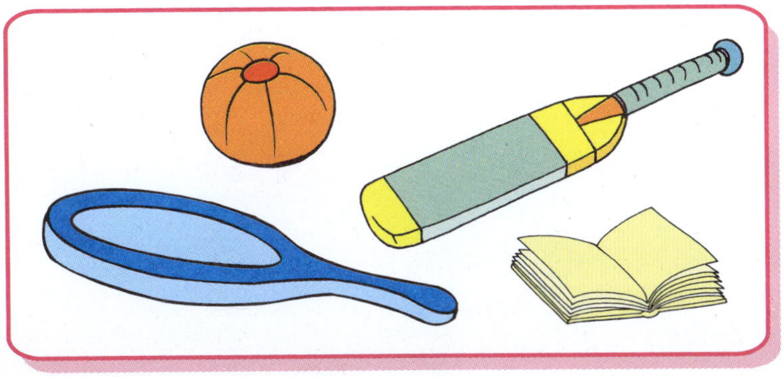

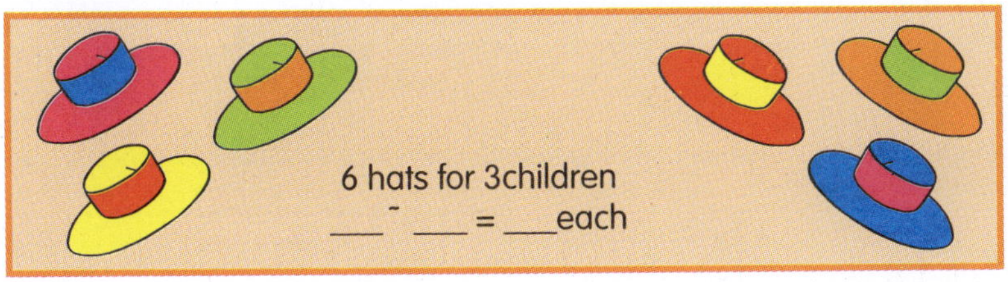

Aiman decided to share his DVDs and hats equally with the children in his neighbourhood. Find out how many items will each child receive.

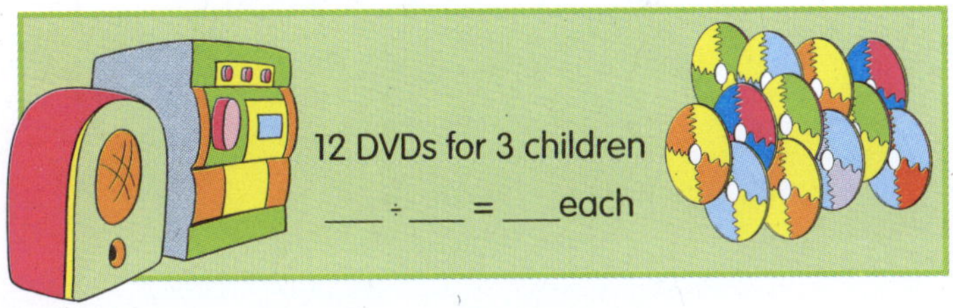

Find the missing number in each sum and match to the answer.

6 + ____ = 11	____ + 16 = 25	17 + ____ = 19

(8) (9) (7) (5) (4) (2)

____ + 8 = 12	9 + ____ = 17	____ + 16 = 23

Colour the animals and match them to their names.

Colour the shapes with corners in red and the shapes with curves in green.

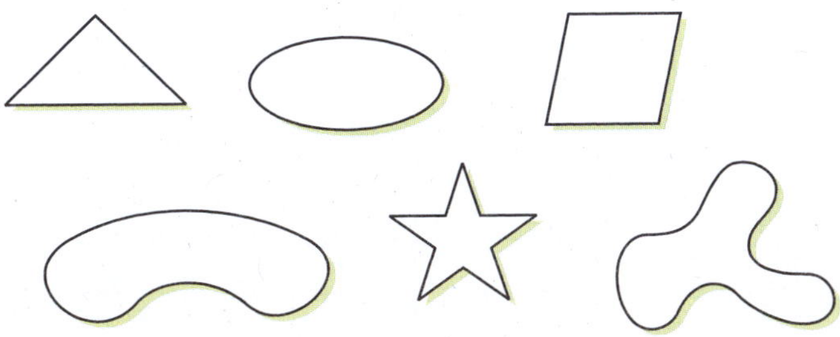

Count the fruits that are damaged.

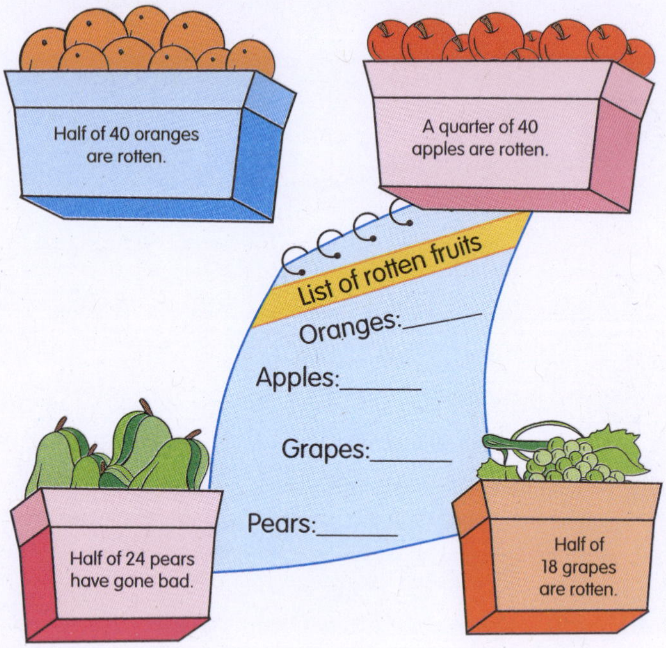

Observe the picture and read the sentences.
Circle the correct sentence.

Trace the letters and practice.

Count and write the total number of snails.

Help Bozo find his bones.

Check and tick who among Marco and Anna has the most objects.

Meransh Myra

Meransh Myra

Meransh Myra

Solve these division sums.

2 ÷ 2 = _____ 24 ÷ 3 = _____ 6 ÷ ______ = 3

8 ÷ 2 = _____ 16 ÷ 2 = _____ 12 ÷ _____ = 6

12 ÷ 3 = _____ 4 ÷ 2 = _____ ______ ÷ 2 = 7

Count the stars and fill in the blanks.

____ groups of 2

____ groups of 4

____ groups of 5

____ groups of 10

Total number of stars.

Colour the odd one in each box.

Unscramble the names of these animals.

Circle the odd one out in each box.

Circle around the straight lines.

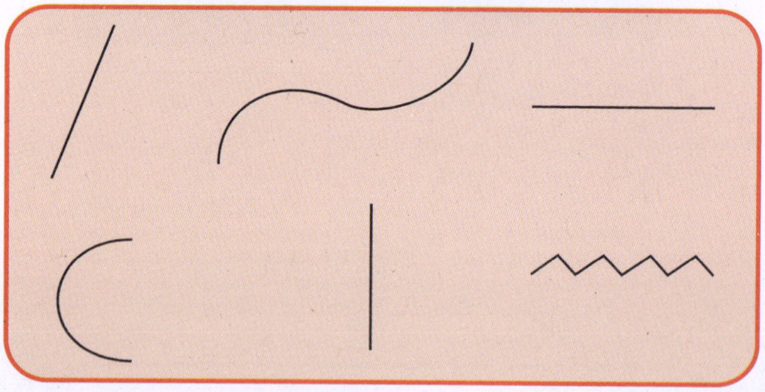

Match each object to its name and colour it.

The last digit of the telephone numbers is the number of the house. Connect the phone to the correct houses.

Trace the letters with a pencil and guess what letter is missing in the words here.

s ___un

t ___ent

Count the balls and form groups of 3. How many groups have you made?

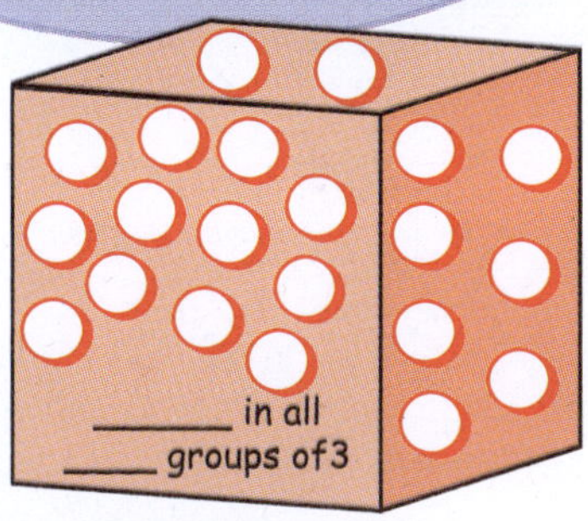

Complete the picture on the right and colour it brightly.

Solve the sum and write the correct answer in the circle below.

Trace number 7.

7	7	7	7	7
7	7	7	7	7

Match the sums to their answers.

Complete the patterns as shown.

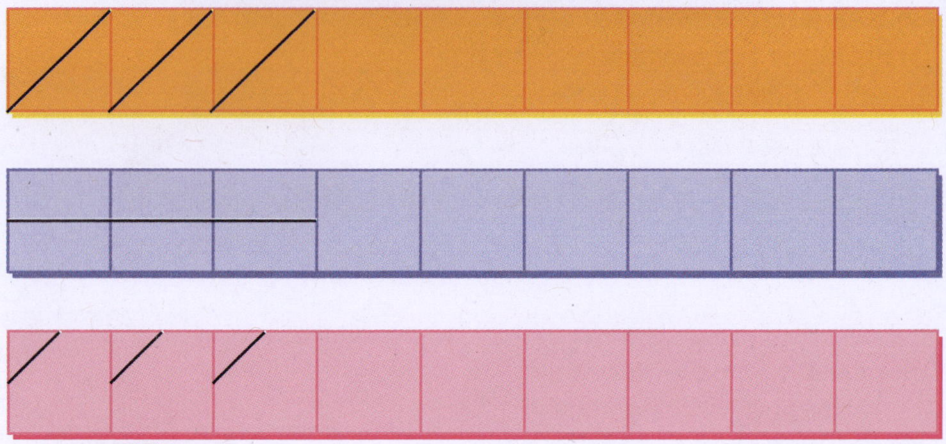

Match the fruits to their names and colour them.

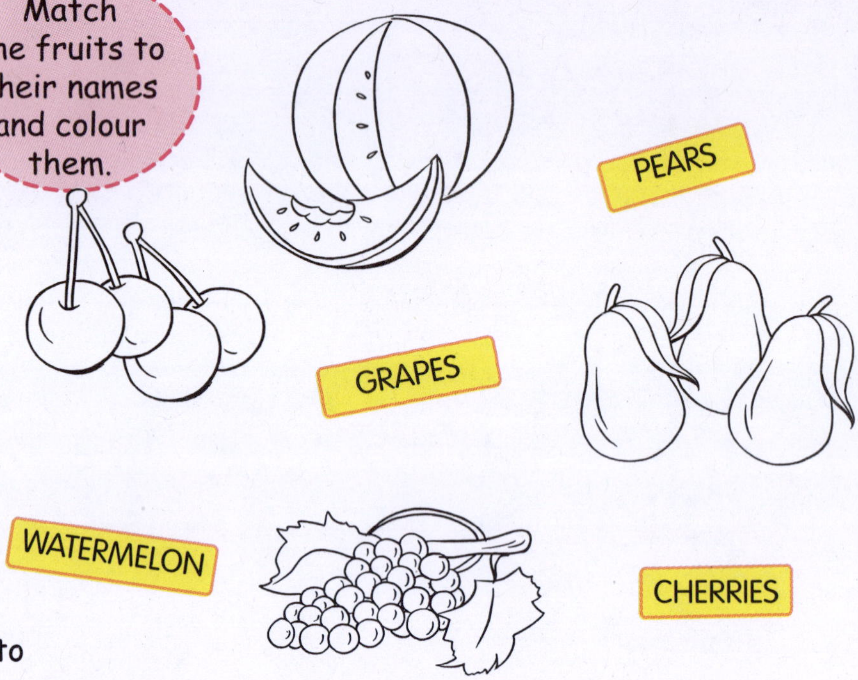

Match equal number of flowers to each vase.

Observe the pictures and read the sentences. Cross the incorrect one.

Count and write the number of objects in each set and colour the pictures.

Match the sums to their answers.

_____ ÷ 10 = 3
63 ÷ _____ = 9
22 ÷ 2 = _____
_____ ÷ 2 = 8

28 ÷ 4 = _____
15 ÷ _____ = 1
16 ÷ _____ = 4
20 ÷ _____ =5

32 ÷ _____ = 8
_____ ÷ 3 = 7
_____ ÷ 4 = 6
27 ÷ 9 = _____

Draw as many circles as indicated.

One

Four

Ten

Eight

Six

Connect the letters according to the alphabetical order.

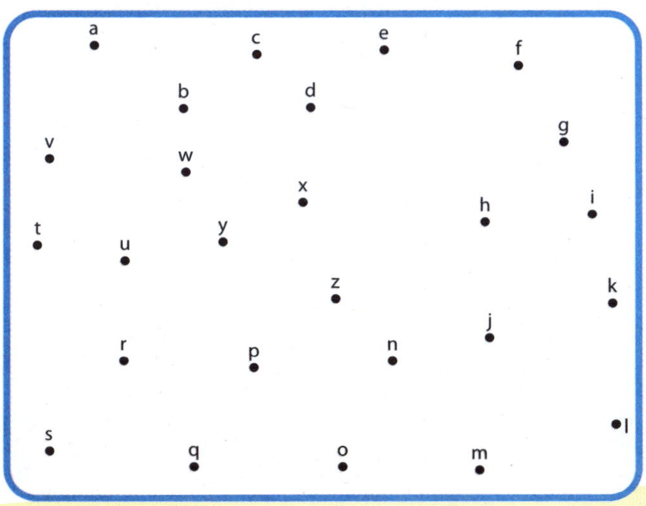

Circle the odd one out.

Solve and fill in the blanks.

Half of 16 = ______

Half of 100 = ______

30 is half______

Half of 50 = ______

______ is half of 6

22 is half ______

Half of 80 = ______

Half of 36 = ______

Parth's sister was 12 years-old two years ago. He is an year younger to her. How old is he? Write.

Dear diary,

How many pieces are there in each jar?

Help Nadeem calculate the time.

Add 5 minutes to find the new time.

2 : 25 → +5 min → 2 : 30

4 : 07 → ______

6 : 37 → ______

10 : 18 → ______

3 : 44 → ______

Look at the pictures and write the letters that is missing from each word.

r Doo_

p Ta_

e H_n

Count the number of objects in each set and also calculate half of it.

half = ____

half = ____

half = ____

How many balloons does Arya need in his hands to make a total of 12?

 +  = 12 balloons

Each dart is placed on a number. Circle the number name.

Five, three, four, six

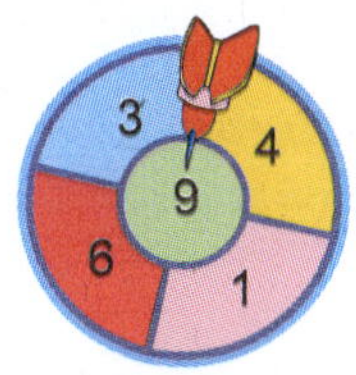

one, six, three, nine

Ten, seven, four, eight

Unscramble and arrange the names of animals in the alphabetical order.

Sehep

____

Senak

____

Srriquel

____

Cwo

____

Match vegetables and fruits to their names. Colour them too.

Help Nadeem solve the sums and write the answers.

What is 9 plus 8?

Add 4, 7 and 5.

What is 11 plus 5?

What is the total of 16 and 7?

Solve the sums and match the answers.

11	50 ÷ 10
5	400 ÷ 10
40	60 ÷ 10
6	110 ÷ 10

Number the animals in correct order as they appear in the food chain.

Help solve these sums.

Add 6 pounds to 3 pounds.

_____ + _____ =

____

_____ + _____ = _____

Is the sum of 3 +4.

_____ + _____ = _____

Match the number, the number name and the correct dots.

seven	1
five	7
nine	3
three	5
one	9

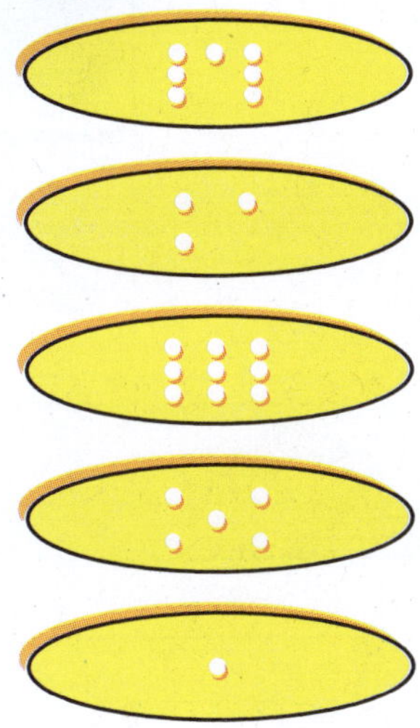

Calculate Kiana's score.

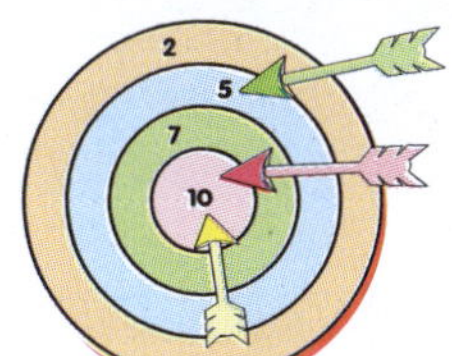

10 + 7 + 5 + 2 = ____

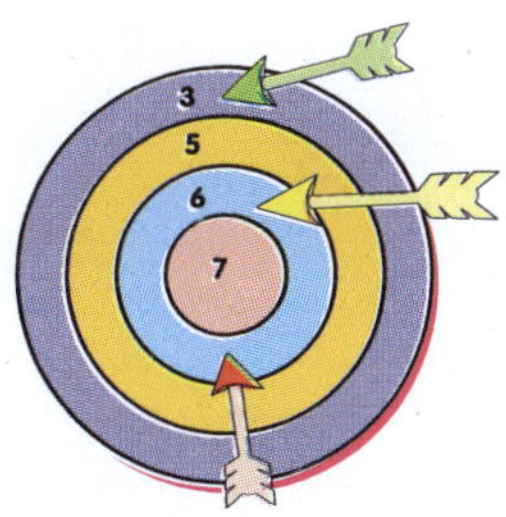

7 + 6 + 5 + 3 =

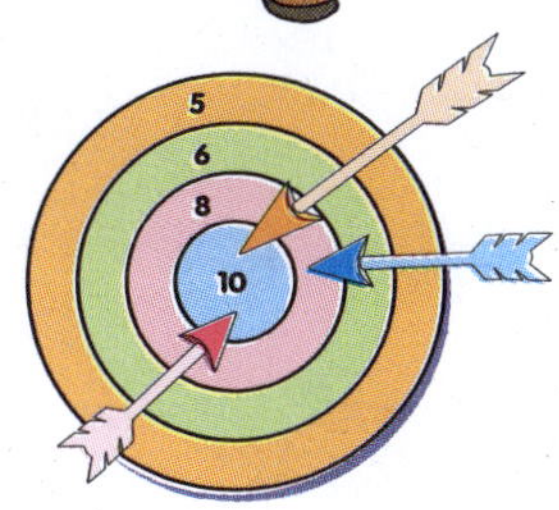

10 + 8 + 6 + 5 =

What is your favourite month? Illustrate it with a drawing.

Aiman decided to share his things equally with the children in his neighbourhood. Find out how many items will each child receive.

16 bats for 4 children

____ ÷ ____ = ____each

10 lollipops for 5 children.

____ ÷ ____ = ____each

Circle the odd one out in each set.

Draw the patterns as shown.

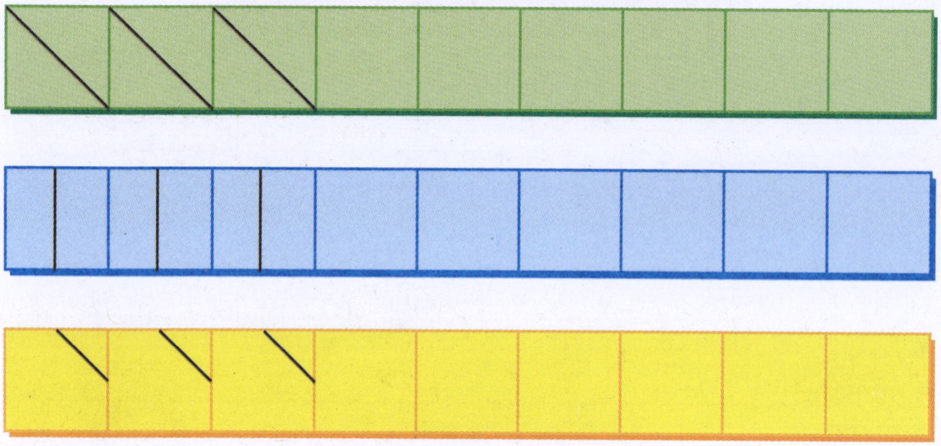

Complete divisions.

Half of 12

12÷2=____

Half of 22

___÷___=___

Count and write the total number of ants.

Netra has to connect each day of the week to the next day. Help her.

The day after

Wednesday	is	Saturday
Friday		Monday
Monday		Wednesday
Thursday		Tuesday
Sunday		Sunday
Tuesday		Thursday
Saturday		Friday

Colour the boxes that add up to 17.

5 + 12	10 + 7	2 + 14	5 + 11
8 + 9	3 + 14	8 + 8	4 + 9
7 + 9	6 + 11	8 + 10	4 + 13
6 + 9			2 + 15

17

Match the opposites. Write them here.

Day -______

Hard - ______

Out-______

Dark - ______

Great - ______

Large - ______

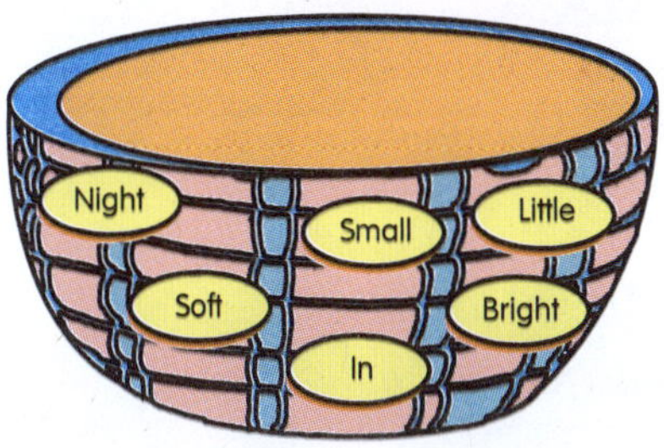

Write the names of these animals in alphabetical order.

______

______

______

______

______

______

Circle all the curves.

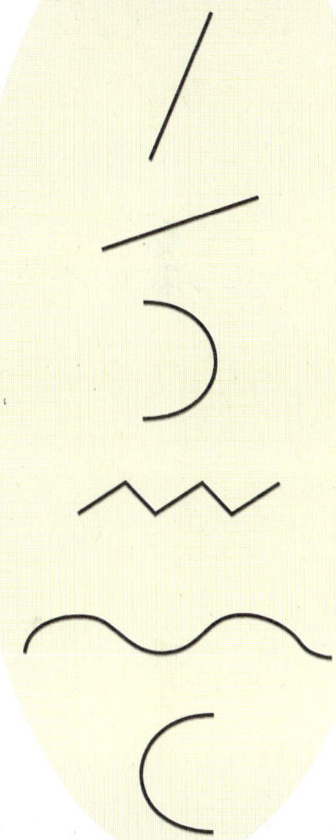

Circle the fourth picture in each row.

Find the results.

7₹ + 2₹ = ______	9₹ + 5₹ = ______
10₹ + 4₹ = ______	6₹ + 3₹ + 2₹ = ______
5₹ + 12₹ = ______	10₹ + 2₹ + 1₹ = ______

Draw a duck and then colour it.

Which of these sets have an even number of objects? Connect them to the word 'pair'

How many sweets does Annie have?

Form different groups:

Marc is playing with Sylvie. Help them divide all the objects into two equal parts.

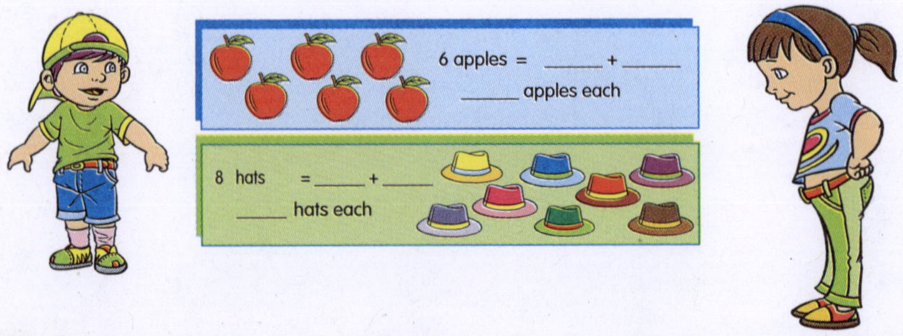

Match all the vegetables with their names. Name which is your favourite vegetable among these.

Connect the dots from 1-50 and colour the picture.

Colour each vegetable and match it to its name.

Circle the items that are made of wood.

Solve the sums and match the answers with the correct corresponding apples.

11 + 7 | 12 + 4 | 4 + 14 | 3 + 9 | 9 + 7 | 9 + 5

3 + 11 | 6 + 10 | 5 + 7 | 3 + 15 | 8 + 6 | 6 + 6

Trace the letters and read the words aloud.

ff office office

dd addition addition

Complete these divisions:

____ ÷ 3 = 7
3 × ____ = 21

____ ÷ 3 = 10
____ × 10 = 30

27 ÷ ____ = 9
9 × ____ = 27

____ ÷ 6 = 6
6 × ____ = 36

15 ÷ ____ = 3
5 × ____ = 15

Colour the animals that lay eggs.

1. Place yourself on START box 30.
   To find the number
2. Divide this number by 2.
3. Divide that number by 3.
4. Add 2 to your answer.
5. Multiply that by 3.

Start

30	2	14	42	3
11	15	6	18	33
35	29	5	67	22
14	1	9	7	10
25	12	16	38	21

Follow the instructions and find the answers.

Solve the sums and match them with corresponding numbers on the cups.

Colour the odd one out in each row.

The last digit of each phone number is the house number. Connect each phone to the correct house.

Solve and write.

How many animals are there per pen? Write the answers in the given circles.

Colour all similar-looking pieces in same colour.

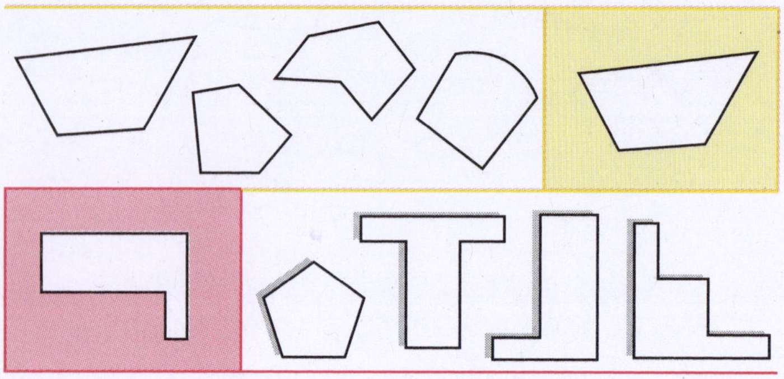

Write the words in alphabetical order: Cheese, Noodles, Doughnut, Sandwich, Rice, Bread, Egg.

__________ __________ __________

__________ __________ __________

____

Connect the dots by counting in tens.

Observe the table carefully and answer the questions.

How many numbers of ?

How many numbers of ?

How many numbers of ?

How many numbers of ?

Tick mark yes or no.

There are two burgers more than the diamonds. yes no

Read the instructions and complete characters.

Colour Jimmy's T-shirt yellow. He wears black shorts and a red cap. Colour the ball he is playing with blue and orange.
Timmy has brown hair. She wears a pink dress with green lines.

Circle the smallest objects in each plate below.

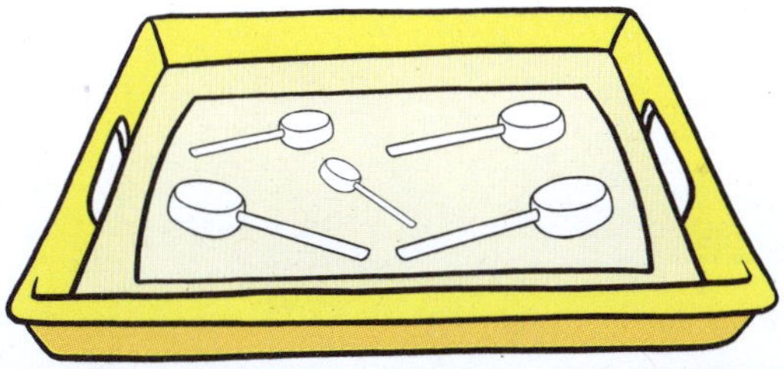

On the board, write the things we should do to keep our city clean. Also draw a picture of a clean and green city that you aspire for.

Write the names of these animals.

 __________  __________

 __________  __________

 __________  __________

Connect the sets with an odd number of objects to the word 'ODD'.

Colour the kites to match the clothes of the child holding it.

Count the number of times the following objects appear.

torch	camera	basket

Draw the carpet and colour it.

In each row colour the pictures and count the number of objects that Meransh and Myra have in total.

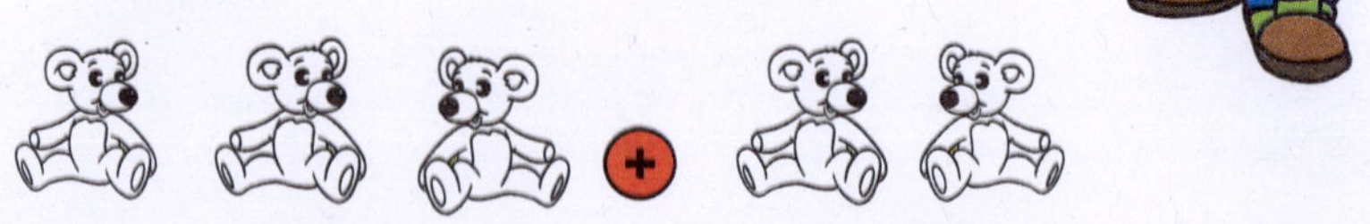

_____ cubs   _____ cubs   _____ cubs in all

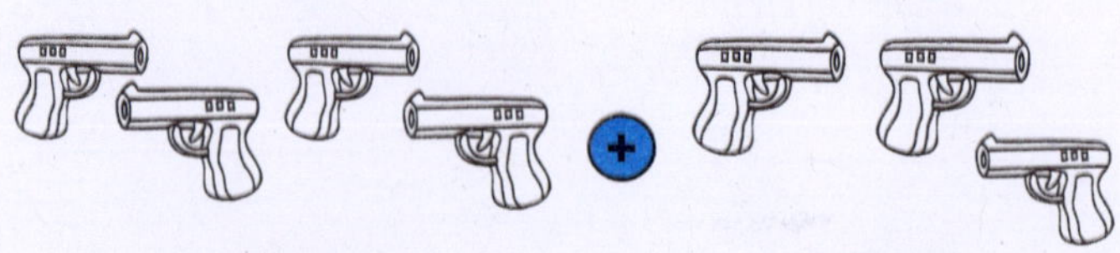

_____ toy guns   _____ toy guns   _____ toy guns in all

Solve the following.

Match these animals to their homes.

Cow

Frog

Hen

Horse

Spider

Rabbit

Dog

Pig

The post office

Ali has 10₹
How much money would he be left with if he buys stamps of ₹ 5 ? ______
How much money would he be left with if he buys stamps of ₹ 2 ? ______

Ali has 30₹
How much money would he be left with if he buys stamps of ₹ 18 ? ______
How much money would he be left with if he buys stamps of ₹ 8 ? ______

Ali has 15 ₹
How much money would he be left with if he buys stamps of ₹ 6 ? ______
How much money would he be left with if he buys stamps of ₹ 4 ? ______

Suppose the Post Office has ₹20, ₹10, and ₹5 stamps, and Ali has ₹30. What value of stamps can he buy?

Write the missing letters in each row.

a __ c __ __ f

h __ j __ l __

__ q r __ __ __

m __ __ p __ r

Match each mode of transportation to it's appointment.

Tractor

Motorcycle

Bicycle

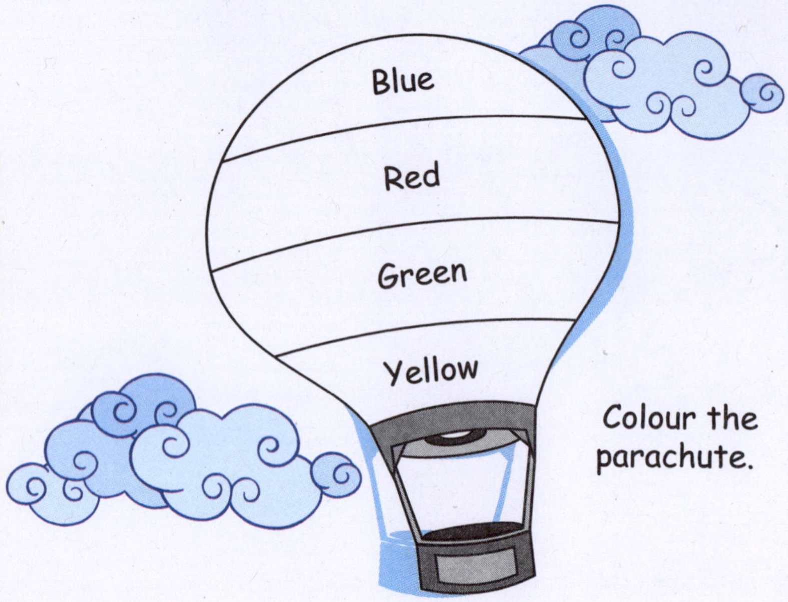

Colour the parachute.

Returns on the dotted lines.

5	5	5	5	5	5	5	5
5	5	5	5	5	5	5	5

Solve the sums.

6 + 5 = ______

11 + 5 = ______

16 + 5 = ______

4 + 11 = ______

5 + 11 = ______

6 + 11 = ______

Number these events in order of their occurrences.

☐ The games at the park

☐ Bedtime

☐ TV

☐ The morning bath

☐ Reading

☐ The school

☐ Dinner

6	6	6	6	6	6	6	6
6							

Trace on the dotted line then writes the number 6 on your own.

Help Sania and Saahil divide these objects into two equal parts.

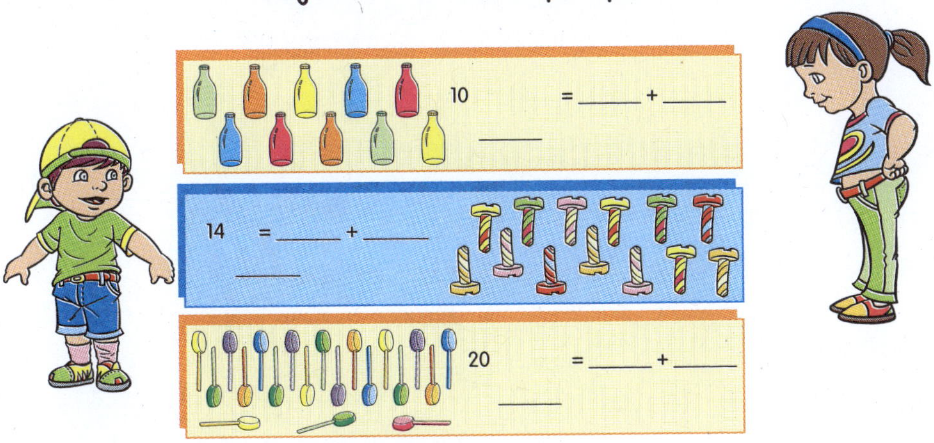

Complete these words.

Colour the identical parts, in each puzzle.

Match each car to its placement in the race.

Second

Fifth

Third

First

Fourth

Trace and colour the car.

Complete these sums.

24 ÷ 4 = _____

4 x _____ = 24

16 ÷ 4 = _____

_____ x 4 = 16

18 ÷ 2 = _____

9 x _____ = 18

Colour the first and last object in each row.

Colour the circles and form groups of 3. How many groups have you formed?

In this drawing, divide each number by 6, then color the house by following the color code.

Put these letters in order to form words. Match each image to its name.

Observe the table carefully and then answer the questions.

How many of  ?

How many of  ?

How many of  ?

How many of  ?

Tick yes or no.

The cars  are more than bikes. 

Yes

No

Colour in the smallest candy in each of the plates.

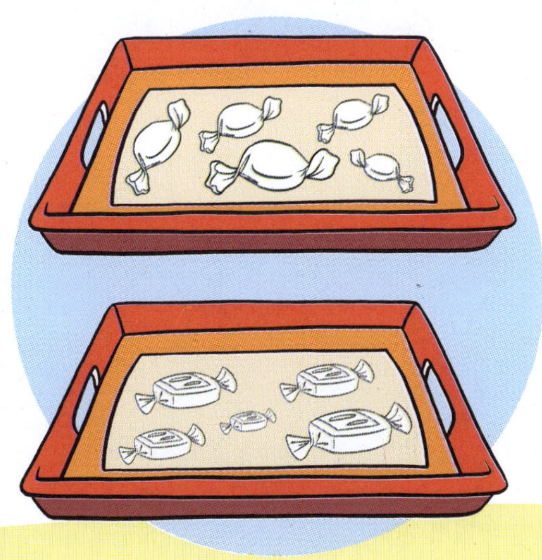

Colour and connect the matching cups and buckets.

Complete these words.

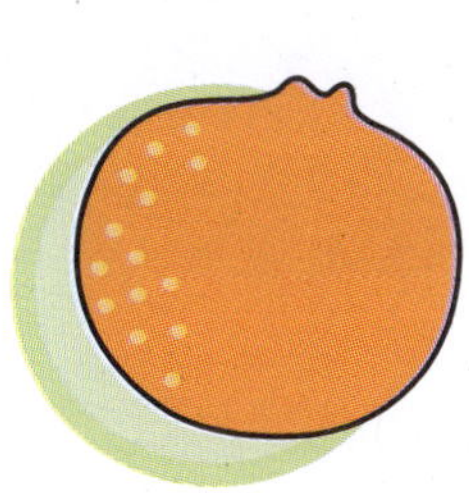

_range

_iwi

Match the identical parachutes.

Help Sarabjit identify all the fruits and colour it.

This butterfly starts from the flower number 1 and continues on its way by adding 5 each time. Trace its course and then colour the flowers it did not visit.

How many triangles can you draw by connecting the dots?

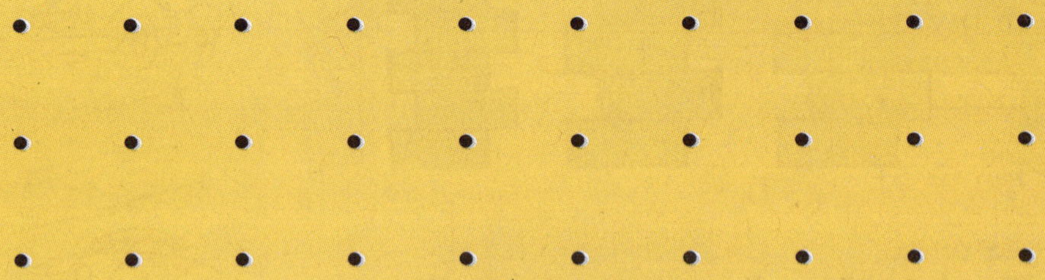

Match the bottles with their correct cork.

Add up the numbers shown on each bottle. The result is the number written on the cork.

Which is the path that will allow Hugo to find his house.

Circle the odd one out in each row.

Help Navjot and Tsering solve the given sums.

Help Ahaan check his addition skills. Tick ✓ right answers and cross ☒ the wrong ones.

6 + 2 = 9	☐	2 + 8 = 9	☐	5 + 6 = 11	☐
3 + 11 = 14	☐	6 + 8 = 13	☐	4 + 12 = 14	☐
10 + 2 = 11	☐	13 + 5 = 18	☐	7 + 3 = 10	☐
4 + 13 = 17	☐	3 + 8 = 11	☐	11 + 3 = 15	☐

What is 2 +4 +3?

____ + ____ + ____ = ____

Add 5 to 4.

____ + ____ = ____

How many triangles can you spot in the figures below?

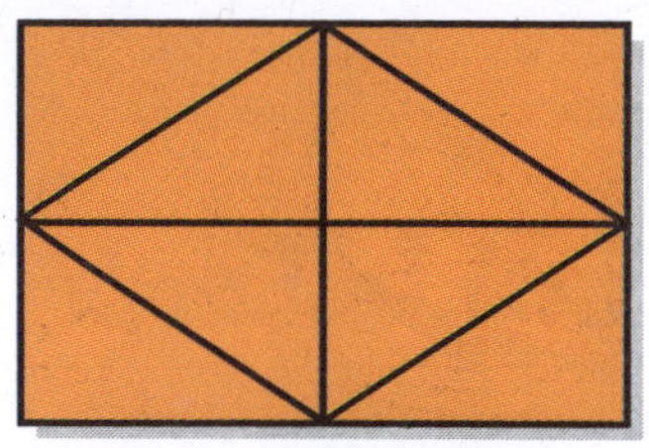

_ _ _triangles

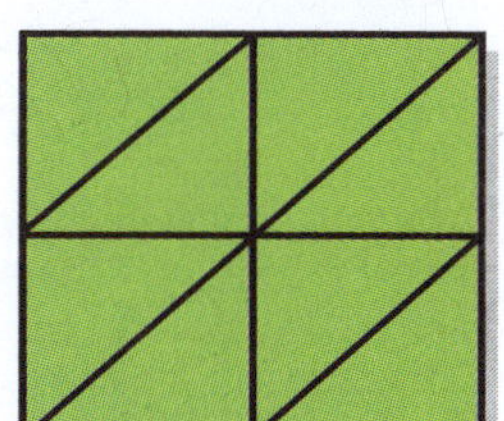

_ _ _triangles

Draw and colour the turtle as shown.

Fill in the blanks and colour.

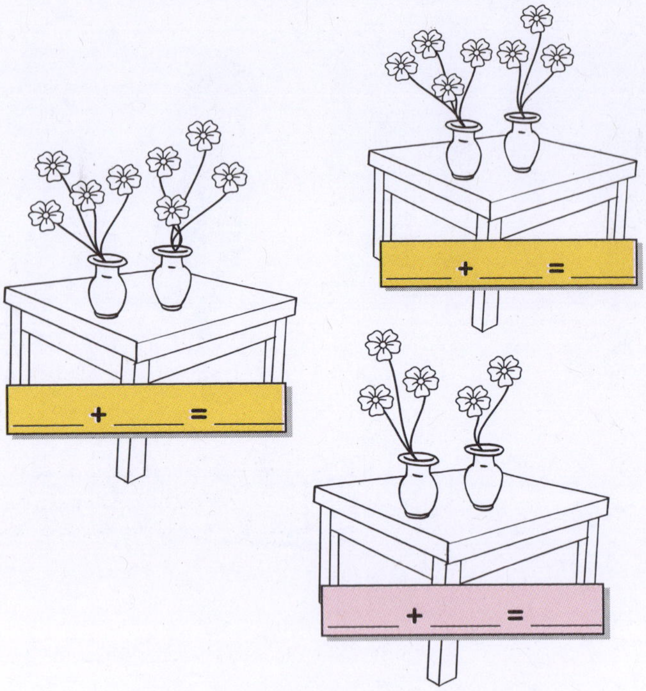

Count the objects and write the results in the white circles.

Match the bottles with their correct cork.

Circle the opposites in each group of sentences.

Billy is happy today. Sam feels sad.

Lucy has curly hair. Marie has straight hair.

Thomas is wearing a black t-shirt. Michel has a white cap.

The glass is on the table is full. My bottle is empty.

Children like to play. Jean and Julien hate dance.

Write words rhyming with these.

Bat | Jug | Book

Circle the black fur animals and find the names of the other animals in the word search.

List of words

- Panther
- Gorilla
- Buffalo
- Wild boar
- Rhino

	W	T	B	S	Y	B	P
A	C	E	Z	A	T	O	A
B	G	X	W	N	A	A	N
I	N	M	Y	G	L	R	T
G	O	R	I	L	L	A	H
Q	P	H	E	I	T	V	E
P	A	I	Z	E	M	X	R
P	F	N	A	R	E	T	E
Z	L	O	B	U	T	H	L
Q	B	U	F	F	A	L	O
C	M	S	G	D	H	S	

Complete words using the letters of the wheel.

ro_e

b_ok

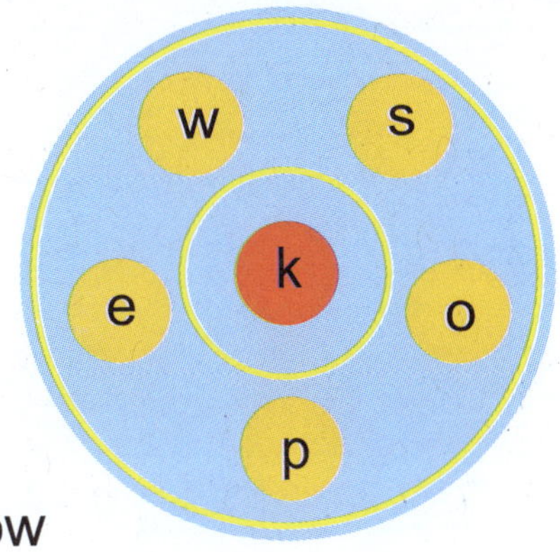

tur_ey

s_at

_indow

_ainting

Colour the second and third object in each row.

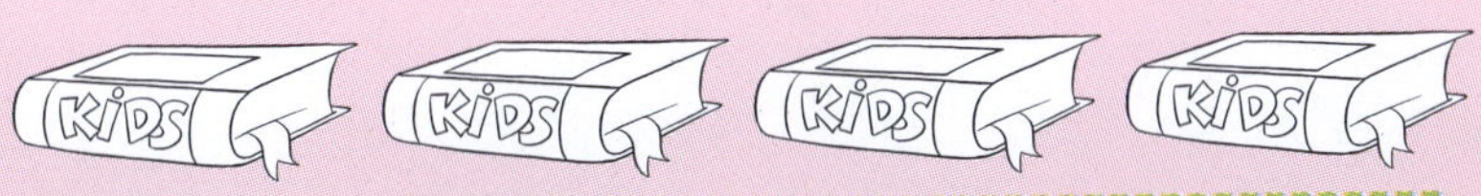

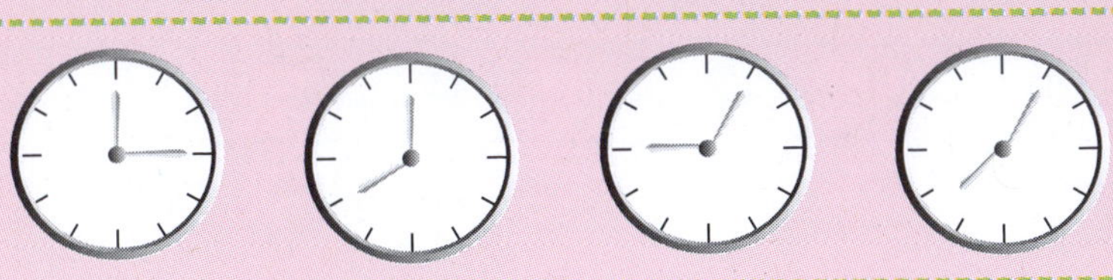

Trace and colour the drums.

Colour in the smallest candy in each of the plates.

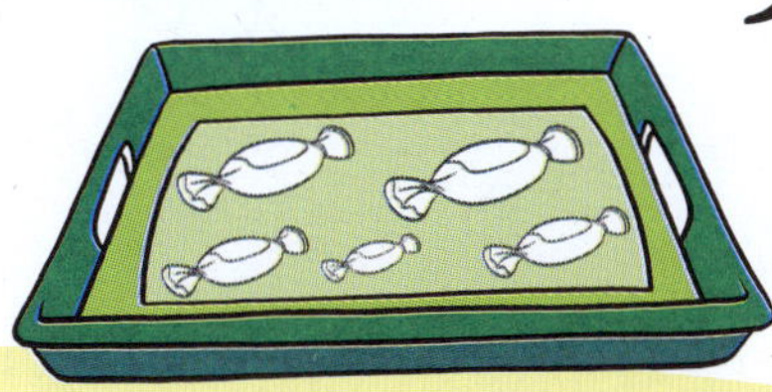

In each set, group and sort three numbers that add up to 20.

2	5	12	3
7	4	3	9

6	7	4	10
2	14	4	5

Use the given clues to identify these animals.

 ______

 ______

 ______

 ______

 ______

 ______

- This animal is very heavy.
- This animal carries her baby in a pouch.

Horse, Rhinoceros, Snail, Frog, Donkey, Polar Bear, Tiger

Lion, Elephant, Giraffe, Kangaroo, Deer, Crocodile, Owl

- It has a long neck.
- She jumps from lily pad to lily pad.
- She stays awake at night.

 ______

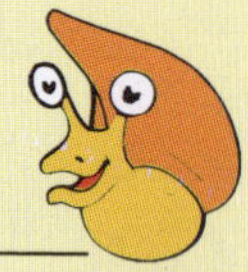 ______

 ______

 ______

 ______

 ______

 ______

 ______

Circle all the sums that add up to 20.

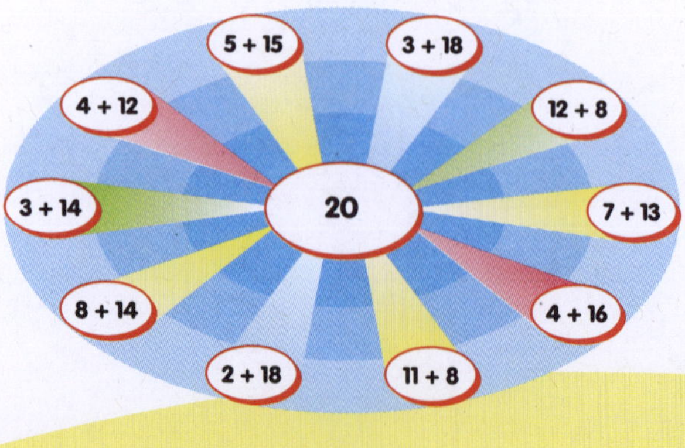

Identify and match the identical pieces of the puzzle.

Connects each lower case letter to its capital.

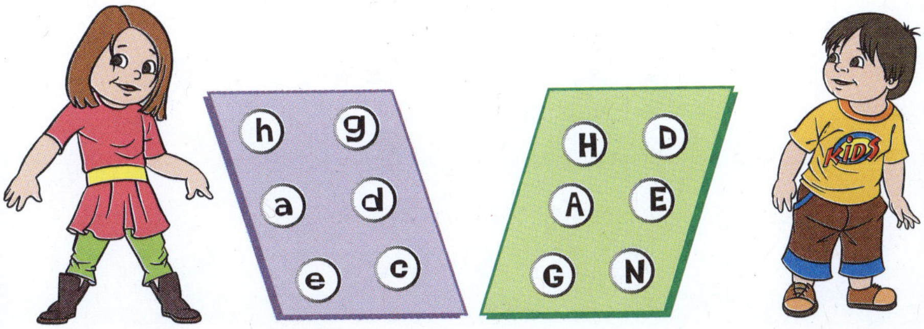

Follow the strings to take each child to its gift.

Trace and write the number 1.

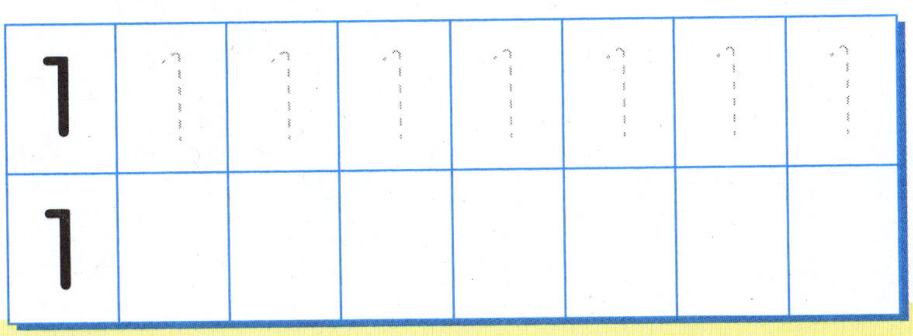

Write the missing letters.

B___lb

___ike

Draw the balloons and colour them.

Write the total number of circles in the given pictures.

Fill in the missing letters to complete the names of the animals. Colour them!

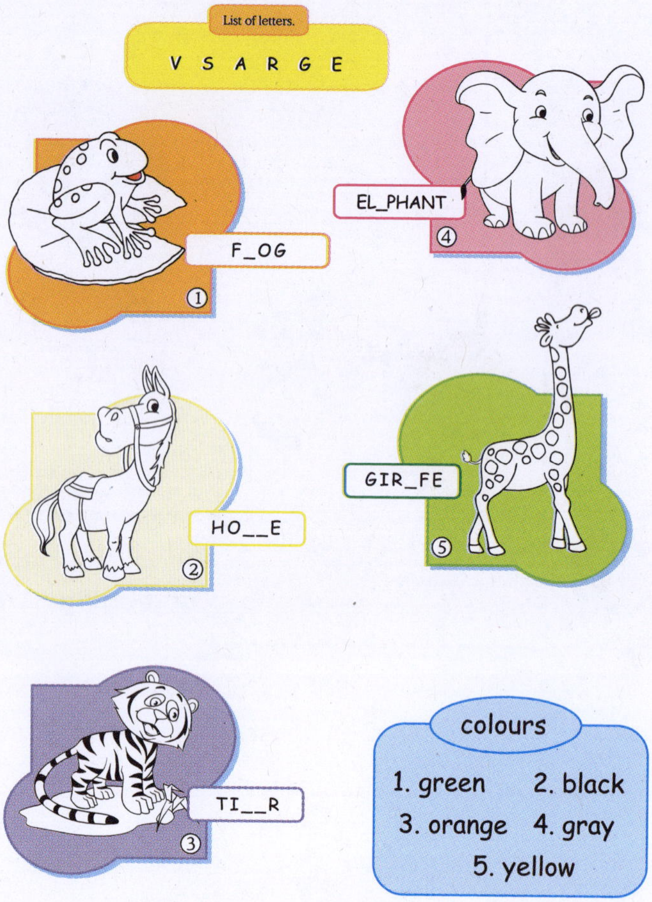

colours

1. green
2. black
3. orange
4. gray
5. yellow

Circle all the objects that you can use on a sports field.

Sam learned his alphabet. He wants you to help him connect identical letters.

Help the bunny add 10 to each stone on which he jumps. Suppose it starts at 1. Trace the path that will lead to carrots.

Match each vehicle to its name.

Ayra mixed numbers. Help her put them back in order.

10 4 9 2 6 3 5 7 1 8

Circle the largest fruit in each tray.

Draw and colour the elephant as shown.

Colour the clothes with your favourite colours.

Count and write down the number of caps and hats in each row.

Put the days of the week in the right order.

Sunday

Friday

Tuesday

Saturday

Thursday

Wednesday

Monday

Thursday | Friday | Monday | Sunday | Wednesday | Tuesday | Saturday

Sarah has prepared an invitation card for his friends. Read it carefully and check the correct answers.

Invitation

You are cordially invited to my party to celebrate my seventh birthday, Tuesday, 24 October, at Town square, at 16:30.

Sarah

- Why did Sarah organise a party?
  - ◯ She moved
  - ◯ It's her birthday.

....

- On which day is the party?
  - ◯ The party will be held on Tuesday, October 24.
  - ◯ The party will be held on Tuesday, November 24.

....

- At what time does the party start ?
  - ◯ The party starts at 15:30.
  - ◯ The party starts at 16:30.

....

- How old will Sarah turn?
  - ◯ She will be 7 years.
  - ◯ She will be 8 years.

Follow the given code on the right to colour the boxes.

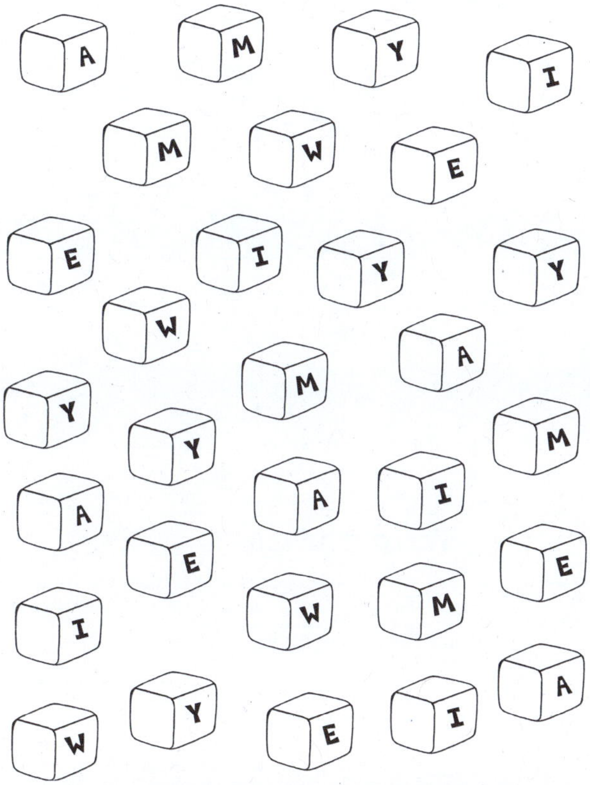

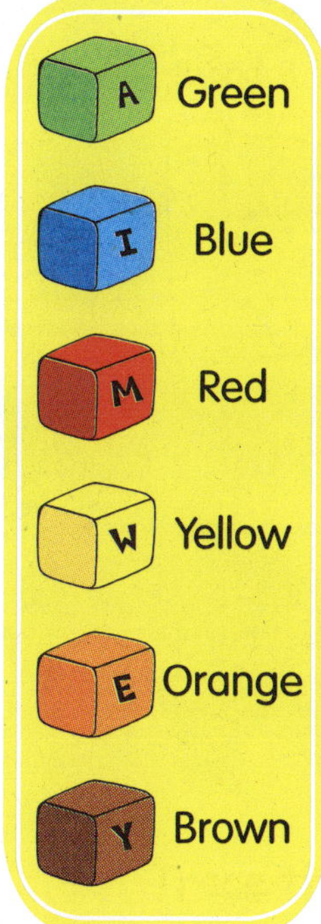

Spot the odd one out.

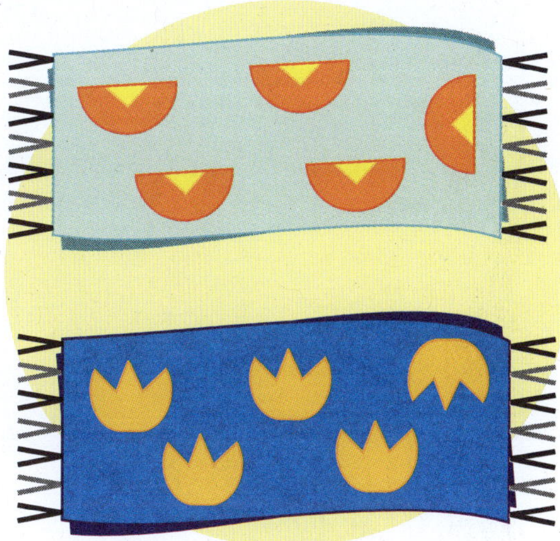

Circle the odd one out in each set

In each row, circle the third object.

Change the vowel (or the first two if any) of each word and write a new word.

fold   word   to

How many flowers are there on every table?

Solve the sums.

16 + _____ = 24

_____ + 12 = 17

4 + 17 = _____

6 + 13 = _____

Draw a crocodile in the box and colour it green.

Write the names of the objects.

1. __________

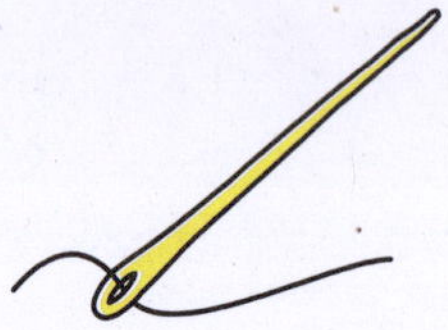

5. __________

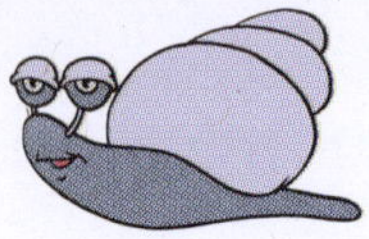

3. __________

4. __________

2. __________

6. __________

Form a word with the first two letters of each of the given word.

bus → bull

street →

hard →

street →

end →

bag →

paw →

evening →

Trace the number and practice.

2	2	2	2	2	2	2	2
2							

Colour the highlighted alphabets that match the ones in the bubble.

B: B D B M A E W B

L: F E L H L Y N X